OXFORD WORL

THE LI
CHRISTINA OF ᴍᴀʀᴋʏᴀᴛᴇ

CHRISTINA OF MARKYATE, daughter of a prosperous Anglo-Scandinavian family, was born in Huntingdon near the close of the eleventh century. At a young age she was taken by her parents on a pilgrimage to St Albans Abbey, where the bearing of the monks made such an impression on her that she made a vow of virginity. Her charm and beauty attracted the unwelcome advances of Ranulf Flambard, bishop of Durham. Christina escaped his clutches, only to find herself forced into a match with a local suitor of Ranulf's choice. How she manages to extricate herself from this situation forms a major theme of the *Life*. After enduring extreme parental pressure to consummate the match, Christina escaped to live as a recluse in some secrecy at Markyate near St Albans. Eventually her marriage was dissolved, paving the way for her to become head of the hermit community at Markyate. It was then that her remarkable friendship began with Geoffrey, abbot of St Albans. Geoffrey provided for all her material needs while Christina became his spiritual mentor. An indication of his affection and esteem for Christina is the adaptation of the St Albans Psalter, one of the glories of twelfth-century English manuscript illumination, for her use.

The *Life* remains something of a mystery, since its author is anonymous and it remains incomplete. Nonetheless it represents a remarkable synthesis of hagiography and romance, relayed with a convincing sense of immediacy.

SAMUEL FANOUS is Head of Publishing at the Bodleian Library. He is co-editor (with Vincent Gillespie) of *The Cambridge Companion to Medieval English Mysticism* (2008).

HENRIETTA LEYSER is a Fellow of St Peter's College, Oxford. She is the author of *Hermits and the New Monasticism* (1984), *Medieval Women: A Social History of Women in England 450–1500* (1995) and co-editor with Samuel Fanous of *Christina of Markyate, A Twelfth-Century Holy Woman* (2005).

OXFORD WORLD'S CLASSICS

For over 100 years Oxford World's Classics have brought readers closer to the world's great literature. Now with over 700 titles—from the 4,000-year-old myths of Mesopotamia to the twentieth century's greatest novels—the series makes available lesser-known as well as celebrated writing.

The pocket-sized hardbacks of the early years contained introductions by Virginia Woolf, T. S. Eliot, Graham Greene, and other literary figures which enriched the experience of reading. Today the series is recognized for its fine scholarship and reliability in texts that span world literature, drama and poetry, religion, philosophy, and politics. Each edition includes perceptive commentary and essential background information to meet the changing needs of readers.

OXFORD WORLD'S CLASSICS

The Life of Christina of Markyate

Translated by
C. H. TALBOT

Revised with an Introduction and Notes by
SAMUEL FANOUS and HENRIETTA LEYSER

OXFORD
UNIVERSITY PRESS

OXFORD

UNIVERSITY PRESS

Great Clarendon Street, Oxford ox2 6DP

Oxford University Press is a department of the University of Oxford.
It furthers the University's objective of excellence in research, scholarship,
and education by publishing worldwide in

Oxford New York

Auckland Cape Town Dar es Salaam Hong Kong Karachi
Kuala Lumpur Madrid Melbourne Mexico City Nairobi
New Delhi Shanghai Taipei Toronto

With offices in

Argentina Austria Brazil Chile Czech Republic France Greece
Guatemala Hungary Italy Japan Poland Portugal Singapore
South Korea Switzerland Thailand Turkey Ukraine Vietnam

Oxford is a registered trade mark of Oxford University Press
in the UK and in certain other countries

Published in the United States
by Oxford University Press Inc., New York

British Library Cataloguing in Publication Data

Data available

Library of Congress Cataloging-in-Publication Data

The life of Christina of Markyate / translated by C.H. Talbot; revised with an
introduction and notes by Samuel Fanous and Henrietta Leyser.
p. cm.
Includes bibliographical references and index.
ISBN 978–0–19–280677–2
1. Christina, of Markyate, Saint, b. ca. 1096. 2. Christian women saints—England—
Biography. I. Fanous, Samuel, 1962– II. Leyser, Henrietta.
BX4700.C567L525 2008
271′.9—dc22
[B]
2007035102

Typeset by Cepha Imaging Private Ltd., Bangalore, India
Printed in Great Britain by
Clays Ltd., St Ives plc.

ISBN 978–0–19–280677–2

1 3 5 7 9 10 8 6 4 2

CONTENTS

INTRODUCTION

CHRISTINA OF MARKYATE was born in the town of Huntingdon in East Anglia some thirty years after the Norman Conquest of England in 1066. Her parents were rich merchants, well-connected and locally esteemed. In the tenth century Huntingdon had been an important centre of Viking occupation, and Christina's father, Auti, was probably of Scandinavian origin. Her mother had the Norman name of Beatrix, a sure indication of the family's aspirations to meld with the new ruling class. Her aunt (whose Anglo-Saxon name of Ælfgifu translated easily into Norman as Alveva) had in this respect been spectacularly successful for she had become the concubine of Ranulf Flambard, right-hand man to King William Rufus (1087–1100) and subsequently bishop of Durham. And had all gone according to plan, Christina might well have taken her aunt's place in Ranulf's bed. How this might have happened, why it did not, and the turnings Christina's life took instead are the subject of one of the most remarkable of twelfth-century saints' Lives.

In 1100, not long after Christina's birth, William the Conqueror's youngest son, Henry, had succeeded his brother William Rufus as king of England. Henry's marriage within a few months of becoming king to Eadgifu, great-great niece of Edward the Confessor (king of England from 1042 to 1066), had created an important link between his lineage and the Anglo-Saxon past. On her marriage Eadgifu had taken the Norman name of Matilda, but this did not stop the royal couple being mockingly referred to by the Anglo-Saxon names of Godric and Godgifu. Against such a backdrop of ethnic tension, the determination displayed by Christina's family to maintain their status in the new Norman world, and their anxiety lest they lose it due to a headstrong daughter, becomes, however unappealing, at least intelligible. Ironically, the path Christina chose, against their wishes, secured greater fame for herself and her family than any sexual liaisons or marriage that they might have hoped to foist upon her.

Christina has often been described as a recluse, that is, as someone who for reasons of religious asceticism has chosen to live an enclosed life, alone or at the most with one or two companions. It is doubtful if this is the best way of under-standing Christina's vocation, since the years when she lived enclosed arose from necessity rather than from choice. The circumstances were these: on an occasion when Ranulf was visiting Ælfgifu (Alveva) his eye alighted on Christina, but Christina, who had already taken a vow of virginity, repulsed his advances. In fury, the spurned bishop determined that Christina be married to a local suitor Beorhtred; her parents, hoping to appease Ranulf, colluded with the plan. At length Christina capitulated, but she steadfastly refused to consum-mate the match, choosing instead to flee close to St Albans, to the protection first of a woman recluse, and then to Markyate to the hermitage of a certain Roger, where she lived in a tiny cell with scarcely room to breathe. Christina tolerated these cramped conditions only because she feared that had her hiding-place been discovered she might have been forced to return to her husband. Once her marriage had been dissolved Christina was free to consider where and how she might live out her vow. Her choice was to return as Roger's heir to Markyate, but she lived now not as a solitary but rather as the head of a small community which gathered about her, and which in 1145 became recognized as a priory.

Christina's life was decisively shaped when she was still a young girl by a pilgrimage she made, together with her parents, to the Benedictine abbey of St Albans. St Albans's renown rested on its possession of the body of Alban, a saint allegedly martyred in England in the early years of the third century and thus with a claim to be England's proto-martyr. Christina visited at a time when the Anglo-Saxon building was being replaced by a bigger and grander Norman abbey—Henry I himself attended its consecration in 1116—but what above all struck the girl, according to her biographer, was the demeanour of the St Albans monks, and it was her desire to emulate their way of life which sparked her determination to take her own vow of virginity and to dedicate her life to God. Such a wish on the part of a young girl need not in itself have been particularly noteworthy or remarkable. Twelfth-century England witnessed a dramatic increase both in the number of men who wanted to become monks or canons and of women who wanted to become nuns. In Christina's home-town of Huntingdon a new priory of canons dedicated to the Virgin had been founded shortly before her birth; during her struggles with her family this community would give Christina considerable support. It is also clear that a significant number of recluses and hermits, both men and women, were at the time living in Christina's neighbourhood. Although the top ecclesiastical posts were by now all filled by Normans (for example, the see of Durham by Ranulf Flambard), local holy men and women continued to minister to people of all ranks. When Christina decided to run away from home it was amongst such people—and with good reason—that her parents first thought to look for her. Ironically, Christina's parents had themselves been away on the day in question on a customary visit to a recluse by the name of Guido, thus giving Christina her chance to slip away unnoticed. Despite their resistance to their daughter's plans to lead the religious life, it would seem, then, that Christina's parents were at the very least conventionally pious, as is evidenced too by that fateful visit to St Albans to seek the protection of the saint 'for themselves and their child' (p. 5). And as a child Christina had certainly imbibed orthodox doctrine, believing, for instance, that Christ was present everywhere and that after death either bliss or torments would await her, depending on how she had conducted herself in this world.

Christina's Marriage

Christina's marriage to Beorhtred, and its subsequent dissolution, lay to rest two ghosts that have long stalked discussions about the lives of medieval women. The first is the assumption that daughters were a nuisance best dumped in a nunnery; in Christina's case this is the one thing her parents very explicitly did not want—such a life of poverty, they argued, would bring their whole family into disrepute. Furthermore—and this despite the fact that Christina had a brother—her parents had high expectations that Christina would and could advance their fortunes in the world: she was, they said:

so shrewd in understanding, so prudent in affairs, so efficient in carrying out her plans that if she had wished to devote herself to things of this world she could have enriched and ennobled not only herself but also all her relatives. To this was added the fact that they hoped that she would give birth to children who would take after their mother. So keen were they on these rewards that they begrudged her a life of virginity. For if she remained chaste for the love of Christ, they feared that they would lose her and all that they could hope to gain through her (p. 21).

The second ghost that needs dispatching is the assumption that women could be forced into marriages against their will. Given the difficulties Christina had in extricating herself from her marriage to Beorhtred, this seemingly unlikely claim needs further explanation.

The theology of marriage was in the twelfth century in a state of flux; in the wake of a spate of ecclesiastical reforms emanating from the papal curia at Rome, canon lawyers were questioning what it was that made a marriage. Throughout the debate the Church continued to adhere to the idea that all that was needed was the consent of the couple concerned; whether this was verbal or written, witnessed or made in private, was beside the point. Controversy, however, broke out as to whether sexual intercourse was essential to seal any such alliance. Various considerations came into play (not least the problem of Mary's perpetual virginity and her marriage to Joseph), but by the end of the twelfth century a compromise had been found and it was agreed that an exchange of marriage vows, made in the present tense, had both legal and sacramental force in themselves. A mere promise to marry, however, was another matter, and in that case there was no marriage unless the promise was cemented by sexual consummation. During Christina's lifetime these issues had yet to be settled, but behind the drama of her relationship with Beorhtred the marshalling of the relevant arguments can already be heard. These were compounded in Christina's case by her own belief in a 'prior contract', in other words, by her belief that in making her vow of virginity she had already become Christ's bride. Time and again this is the argument she uses to fight her corner. 'Tell me,' she asks Beorhtred, 'tell me . . . if another were to come and take me away from you and marry me, what would you do?' Beorhtred replied, 'I wouldn't put up with it for a moment as long as I lived. I would kill him with my own hands if there were no other way of keeping you.' To which Christina answered: 'Beware then of wanting to take to yourself the Bride of Christ lest in his anger he slay you' (p. 23). Although the trope of becoming a Bride of Christ went back to the days of the early Church, Christina's use of the image carries it beyond the metaphorical and foreshadows a new literalness in the way in which holy women came to talk about their God. In important ways, such marriages (between holy women and Christ) were intimately connected with Eucharistic devotion and with the belief (confirmed at the Lateran Council of 1215) in Christ's real presence in the host. Ecstatic reception of the host is most usually associated with continental mystics such as Hadewijch of Brabant (early thirteenth century) or Catherine of Sienna (1347–80), but Christina too evidently communicated frequently, and when she did she would become 'rapt', caught up in the contemplation of God and unaware of anything else that was going on about her. Significant in any discussion of such 'rapture' is that the Song of Songs, long read as an allegory of the marriage between God and the Church, was in the twelfth century being interpreted as a love-song between God and the individual soul. A copy of the eighth-century commentary of Bede on the Song of Songs, made at St Albans in the early twelfth century and which Christina might well have known, presents an early example of this new interpretation, depicting as it does the bride and groom as lovers about to kiss rather than as stiffly hieratic figures.

The Monastic Options

Once her marriage to Beorhtred had been dissolved Christina was at liberty to decide how and where she might want to lead the religious life. Whereas the suggestion of the *Life* that the archbishop of York considered sending her to France to the newly established monastery of Fontevrault or to the famed house of Marcigny may be no more than rhetorical panache, the twelfth century, as mentioned already, undoubtedly witnessed the rapid development of a monastic renaissance across Europe, so that even within Christina's own lifetime opportunities for women (and for men) who wanted to join religious communities had multiplied rapidly. In England alone between 1130 and 1165 at least eighty-five new communities for women were founded, many by women themselves, and the monastic monopoly hitherto exercised by the Benedictine order was forever broken. Women might, for example, now adopt the customs of some of the new orders of monks, such as those of the Cistercians, who argued that they were returning to a purer form of monasticism that over the centuries had become sullied; or they might join the one English order ever to have been founded, that of the Gilbertines, who were reviving the notion of a double monastery, made up in this case of nuns and canons. If we are to believe her *Life*, Christina chose to return to Markyate both because of her veneration for St Alban and because of her former friendship with Roger, who by then had been buried in the abbey. At some point, too, Christina's sister Margaret joined her at Markyate, while their brother Gregory became a monk of St Albans. We do not know the circumstances of these conversions on the part of Christina's siblings, but the *Life* hints that at some point her parents fell on hard times, and that whereas before they had feared that her life of poverty would disgrace the whole family, now Christina's community at Markyate was their one anchor in an uncertain world. The original anxieties felt by Christina's parents were not, however, groundless: many of the new communities founded in the twelfth century failed to secure the financial backing to survive; it was the generosity displayed towards Christina by Abbot Geoffrey of St Albans that made it possible for Markyate to flourish (though the actual land was given by St Paul's of London).

Christina's Spirituality

When she was a young child Christina used to say private prayers out loud to Christ, 'as if he were a man whom she could see' (p. 4). On being teased for this she broke the habit, but her sense of the immediate presence of God and her ability to visualize and experience him in human terms never left her.

Not only was she Christ's bride—and who, she asks, could possibly have found a wealthier husband? (p. 18)—she could also be his nursemaid, as on the occasion when he visited her as a child: 'in the guise of a small child, he came to the arms of his sorely tested spouse and remained with her a whole day, not only being felt but also seen. The maiden took the child in her hands, gave thanks, and pressed him to her bosom' (p. 48). The intimacy which Christina felt towards Christ bears witness to the well-attested development in the twelfth century of a Christocentric piety focused on the merciful Saviour of the New Testament rather than on the avenging God of the Old. While the most notable exponents of this new form of piety were the Cistercians, its first flowering in England is indebted to Anselm, archbishop of Canterbury (d. 1109), whose prayers and meditations were widely sought and extensively circulated. Numerous links between Canterbury and St Albans make highly likely an Anselmian contribution to the spirituality of St Albans, but in Christina's case her sense of the humanity of God may also have been influenced by current developments in drama. Scholars have drawn attention to the rich implications of these possibilities, and to the connections between what is known of contemporary liturgical drama and certain scenes from Christina's *Life*. In the history of the theatre in England St Albans in any case holds a special place, since when Geoffrey (later abbot and Christina's patron) first came to England from Le Mans he put on a play about St Katherine—the first play of its kind known to have been performed in England—for which he borrowed copes from St Albans. When fire broke out in his house the copes were burnt, and in recompense Geoffrey gave himself to St Albans as a 'burnt offering'. It may, then, be no coincidence that in Christina's *Life* episodes are constructed time and time again in highly dramatic terms, culminating in the appearance of a certain 'pilgrim' (p. 83) whom Christina longs to see and entertain, and who announces by way of his mysterious disappearance his identity as Christ. In her dealings with this 'pilgrim' Christina is enabled to 'become' both the Mary whom Christ visits at Bethany and one of the disciples who accompanied him on the road to Emmaus. The correspondence between the scenes depicting the Emmaus story in the St Albans Psalter, Christina's experience as described in the *Life*, and with what is known of the 'stage' instructions for the presentation of the Easter plays now coming into vogue across Europe, compellingly illustrates the ways in which literal and emotional seeing could intermesh.

Although Christina's marriage to Christ lies at the heart of her vocation, her devotion to his mother Mary is equally marked. In her home town of Huntingdon, in the difficult days before her escape, it is 'the memory of the Mother of God' (p. 11) and the Hail Mary prayer which give her the courage to defy her parents, and throughout her life it is Mary who comes to her aid, as, for example, when the Virgin terrifies Beorhtred into finally releasing Christina from her vows to him; and it is Mary as queen of heaven, 'seated upon a throne [with] gleaming angels seated about her' (p. 43), who promises to give Christina anything for which she cares to ask. Devotion to the Virgin was strong in late Anglo-Saxon England. Here the controversial doctrine of the Immaculate Conception of the Virgin found powerful advocates, a doctrine that at least some Norman ecclesiastics (among them abbots of St Albans) later took up and championed. Thus it is hardly likely to be a coincidence that Christina is recorded as having died on 8 December, in other words, on the Feast of the Immaculate Conception.

Christina is not herself described as spotlessly pure: not only does she, in a moment of weakness, agree to be married to Beorhtred, she also, and more significantly, acknowledges the lustful desires aroused in her by the man with whom she took refuge after the death of Roger and before being able to return to Markyate. (The *Life* tactfully conceals the man's identity.) Although Christina was able in the man's presence to exercise self-control, 'in his absence she used to be so inwardly inflamed that she thought the clothes which clung to her body might catch fire' (p. 47). The narrative makes it very clear that never at any moment did Christina succumb to the temptations the situation presented, but nonetheless when she came to make her solemn profession the memory of the experience was such that Christina was forced to wonder whether she could properly claim virginal status: 'For she remembered the forcefulness of thoughts and the stings of the flesh with which she had been troubled, and even though she was not aware of having fallen either in deed or desire, she did not dare assert that she had escaped unscathed from such great storms' (p. 53). In the light of twelfth-century theological debates on the nature of sin, intention, and contrition, this is a passage noteworthy in its suggestion that Christina (or the author of her *Life*) possessed a highly scrupulous and sophisticated conscience that would have no truck with earlier concepts that placed weight on deeds rather than on intentions. Remarkable too is the manner in which God tells Christina that Christ has indeed preserved her chaste in both mind and body. No priest mediates; she receives instead direct reassurance from heaven, and with it confirmation of her own authority as angels place on her head a crown from which two white fillets hung down 'like those of a bishop's mitre' (p. 54). Despite the official teaching of the Church in the Middle Ages that prohibited women from exercising priestly functions, this vision makes it clear that women might feel themselves sufficiently empowered to receive mandates directly from God.

Christina and Friendship

Friendship is a significant theme in the *Life* of Christina, as it was in monastic circles throughout the twelfth century. Christina's *Life* presents friendship in its various guises. It is not an unproblematic good: friends are not always what they seem; they may be fickle (as, for example, is the canon Sueno, who for a time loses his trust in Christina), and they may be downright dangerous (as, for example, is the anonymous 'protector' who had aroused such feelings of desire in Christina), but at their best, friends support and enrich each other's spiritual lives. Thus, when Christina first goes to live in Roger's hermitage at Markyate Roger is wary of making any contact with her, but a mutual glance exchanged by chance between them when they are both in Roger's chapel inspires each with such trust that thereafter they become close friends: 'through their dwelling together and encouraging each other to strive after higher things, their holy affection grew day by day, like a large flame springing from two burning brands joined together' (p. 40). But the closeness of their relationship was not without its problems. In the years she spent with Roger, Christina was still technically a married woman; even without this complication there would have been many ready to gossip about their intimacy. Years later, after Roger's death, when Christina has returned to Markyate and is now heavily dependent on the Abbot Geoffrey of St Albans for material support, the same problem continues to beset her. There could be no avoiding the fact that close spiritual relationships between a man and a woman caused tongues to wag. The occasional sexual scandal, such as the infamous case of the pregnant nun of the newly founded Gilbertine house of Watton (the Gilbertines being the order that had established 'double houses' for both sexes), confirmed a deeply held belief that nothing good was likely to come out of close associations between men and women. Nonetheless, despite such anxiety, from the twelfth century onwards the number of spiritual friendships between men and women grew apace. For this, the *Life* of Christina, particularly in its description of Christina's relationship with Geoffrey, provides compelling evidence.

The *Life* of Christina illustrates two strands in twelfth-century theology that can help explain this new emphasis and value placed on friendship. The first is an insistence on the humanity of God, on a God who even now might make himself known in human form, whether as a baby (p. 48) or as a handsome young man (p. 84); the second—closely linked— is the insistence that in loving each other men and women come to share in God's salvific plan. Christina realizes this, even to excess; on one occasion she needs a vision to remind her 'that there was only one thing in which a person should not place another before him or her self and that was God's love' (p. 83). Such themes are explored also in Cistercian writing of the time, notably in the work of Ailred of Rievaulx, a writer perhaps known to Christina through their shared friendship with Thurstan, archbishop of York. Ailred's concern is with friendships among men; but in fact, from the twelfth century onwards, it is friendships between holy men and women that assume particular importance. Given the ever-lingering fear of sexual temptation, this needs some explanation.

As Christina's *Life* shows, a woman might have some special access to God that was barred to a man. It is unlikely to be a coincidence that this belief took hold at precisely the moment when new forms of professionalism and careerism in the running both of Church and State were emerging and causing a degree of moral panic. Emblematic of this is the appearance at the court of Henry I (and it is Henry who would have been king when Christina and Geoffrey first met) of a new system for counting money—the abacus—and that it is from Henry's reign that we have for the first time the country's finances set out in a Pipe Roll. At the same time, the foundation of schools (nascent universities) offered a form of education to men, though not to women, that caused anxiety: the consequences that had followed from Adam and Eve's eating of the apple from the Tree of Knowledge was an ever-present reminder of the dangers of intellectual curiosity. In this climate direct access to God, unmediated through books and untainted by worldly ambition, was of inestimable value. Time and again this access is what Christina has to offer Geoffrey. Even before they meet Christina manages, through supernatural power, to dissuade Geoffrey from undertaking some unsuitable and costly project; thereafter the abbot promises to 'give up everything unlawful, to fulfil her commands, and that he would himself be the patron of her hermitage. All he asked was her intercession with God' (p. 59). And he was as good as his word. Whenever he was tempted to sin, the thought of Christina held him back; when he is called away on royal or ecclesiastical business Christina sees to it that he does not have to go, and he is left in no doubt that 'the purity of the virgin had more power with God than the factious and shrewd cunning of the great ones of this world' (p. 74). How it is that Christina can foresee the future and knows everything he does without his telling her does indeed puzzle Geoffrey (and even gives him sleepless nights), but it confirms him in his desire to spend time with her and to help her community; thus, 'while he busied himself in supplying the maiden's needs, she strove to enrich the man in virtue' (p. 68).

Christina as a Visionary

Christina's visions can in the main be said to fall into three overlapping categories: ecstatic, consolatory, and prophetic.

Ecstatic visions occur when Christina was 'rapt' (the word echoes the experience of St Paul in the New Testament) and gave herself up 'to the contemplation of the countenance of her creator' (p. 68). Such visions might be characterized by feelings of extreme ardour or by a sense of the 'sweetness' of God's presence, but they are often imageless, in contrast to many of Christina's other visions which are notable for their vivid pictorial qualities. Moments of ecstatic contemplation were, the *Life* suggests, the fruits of long training given to Christina during the years when she was living with Roger. Every evening Roger would free Christina from the tiny cell in which she had to spend the day and take her with him into his chapel, where he would train her in the art of prayer, both by word and example. On these occasions Christina learnt 'secrets that are hardly credible' (p. 41).

Christina's consolatory visions begin during the period when she is struggling to free herself from her marriage to Beorhtred. Her first vision is in fact preceded by a vision granted to a Jewess who has been brought in by Christina's mother to try to bewitch her; the Jewess sees that any such attempt will be in vain, since Christina is protected by two ghostly persons, dressed in white. Shortly after this, Christina has a highly complicated dream-vision in which she is introduced to the Virgin, who promises a tear-stained Christina help and deliverance, a promise guaranteed as the vision unfolds by the sight of Beorhtred, prostrate and swathed in black unsuccessfully attempting to seize Christina, dressed in white, as she passes by him. When Christina wakes and finds that her pillow is wet with actual tears, she concludes that this was no illusionary dream but rather a promise of real help to come. And as already seen, at other key moments throughout the *Life* the Virgin does indeed come to Christina's aid.

From the point of view of Abbot Geoffrey the most important of Christina's visions are those which serve to demonstrate her powers of second-sight, since it is this, as mentioned previously, which inspires the trust Geoffrey comes to place in her. 'Through the prompting of the spirit' Christina knows time and again what Geoffrey is about to do, while her visions serve to validate her control over him. Thus she sees Geoffrey cemented in a wall (p. 72), ringed around by a fence (p. 73), and locked in an embrace strengthened for her by Christ folding his hands over hers (p. 76). To a considerable extent, Christina's ability to foresee what will happen depends on her petitioning God for whatever it is she wants, either for herself or for Geoffrey, and in this sense she herself creates future events. If her prayers are answered she knows by certain signs such as a bird 'fluttering . . . within her breast' or the sight of 'one [or] more often three lights shining with equal brilliance and splendour' (p. 77). Chillingly, Christina's power is further illustrated by her ability to cause sudden death or illness to those who cross her; but then it would be a mistake, never made in the Middle Ages, to confuse holiness with meekness.

The St Albans Psalter

The psalms of the Old Testament were central to the prayer life of any medieval holy man or woman. When she had first run away from home, and was in hiding in Flamstead, Christina is portrayed reading and singing psalms day and night. So irritated were various devils by this that they turned themselves into toads 'with big and terrible eyes' and squatted on the middle of the psalter 'which lay open on the lap of the Bride of Christ for her use at all hours' (p. 38). Years later, when Christina was at Markyate under the protection of Abbot Geoffrey, the St Albans Psalter, widely acknowledged as one of the most splendid of all English Romanesque manuscripts, was in all probability adapted for her use so as to

make it a fit present from Geoffrey to Christina. The minia-
ture for Psalm 105 (unusually, pasted in rather than painted
on the page) that depicts a woman, thought to be Christina
herself, stretching out her hand towards God as four monks
cluster behind her, may perhaps mark the moment when the
book (already in the making) changed direction and became
hers. Apart from the psalms, the book contains three other
sections: a calendar; forty full-page miniatures depicting the
Fall of Man and the lives of Christ, St Martin, and David;
and finally the *Life of St Alexis* together with three full-page
miniatures of the Emmaus story. The Alexis story—the first
known piece of literature written in Old French to have
survived—has been seen as having particular relevance to
Christina, given that it is in part the account of an unconsum-
mated marriage. It is certainly a story with which Christina is
likely to have been familiar, since St Albans had a chapel dedicated to Alexis which Ranulf, bishop of Durham, had consecrated, very probably at a time when he would also have visited
Christina's aunt. Meanwhile, the miniatures in the Psalter of
the Emmaus story can be related to Christina's visions of the
handsome pilgrim who visited her at Markyate. Of even
greater significance, however, for proof of the book's owner-
ship is the evidence from the calendar, where there are listed
not only a carefully chosen selection of feasts of women saints
and of saints that belonged to Christina's home-lands, but
most conclusively of all, entries that commemorate the deaths
of her family and her friends—her mother and father, brothers and sisters, Abbot Geoffrey and Roger the hermit.

The Life *and Hagiography*

Hagiography is not and was never intended to be biography
in the modern sense of the word. The hagiographer's concern
is with symbolic truth rather than historical reality; it was,

therefore, perfectly in order to represent saints performing 'copycat' miracles, taken from the lives of other saints, since this helped the reader or listener to identify recognized patterns of sanctity. The hagiographer's audience would also have known that meaning is always complex, since it was accepted that Scripture needed to be understood on at least three levels, the literal, the allegorical, and the anagogical (Jerusalem, for example, is at the same time an actual city, a symbol for the Church on earth and for the heavenly city). Saints' lives might similarly be multilayered. At first glance Christina's *Life* might suggest that it presents an exception, and indeed the original editor, C. H. Talbot, who first edited and translated the text in 1959, praised it for being a seemingly realistic story, 'refreshingly unconventional' and short on miracles. While historians have since become more sympathetic towards the miraculous, Christina's *Life* is for the most part still regarded as unusually free from the conventional topoi found in hagiographical texts. But the quaint and homely sayings the author attributes to Christina, such as the proverb 'white stones will be thrown into the pot' (p. 64), all too easily disguise the learning that underpins the *Life* and the familiarity of the author with a range of texts—both biblical and patristic—as well as his sensitivity to the dramatic potential which Christina's story presented. Recent critical readings now emphasize that 'straight' readings of the text in fact do an injustice to the sophistication of the author. Christina's *Life*, deeply rooted though it is in a medieval English landscape, remains heavily indebted both to the basic structures of saints' lives of antiquity and to the newly awakened fascination with vernacular romance, with its motifs of disguise and escape, the use of dialogue, and attention to dramatic detail.

Significant puzzles about the *Life* nonetheless remain: who was the author, and for whom and when was he writing?

Reference to St Albans monastery as 'his', makes it highly probable that he was a St Albans monk; certainly he was someone who knew Christina well and had had many conversations with her. Much less easy to ascertain is when he was writing, whether before or after Christina's death, and whether he ever finished his task. The *Life* as we have it is clearly incomplete, breaking off as it does in mid-sentence. Why should this be? As the Note on the Text explains, Christina's *Life* is to be found at the end of a fourteenth-century manuscript, badly damaged by fire in the eighteenth century. While an examination of the manuscript makes it clear that it does indeed lack pages, this does not itself prove that the fourteenth-century scribe had before him a finished *Life* of Christina. It is possible to argue that the scribe was himself copying out an incomplete text even if he had before him rather more than is extant today.[1] This argument is based in part on the discussion of the text by a seventeenth-century scholar who had seen the text before the fire, and in part on an account of Christina to be found in the *Deeds of the Abbots of St Albans*; this account, which may have been based on a different version of the *Life* of Christina which has not survived, was possibly also incomplete. If there were indeed two versions of the *Life*, both unfinished, this may be a clue as to the bigger mystery of why there is no evidence, beyond the merest whisper, for any cult of Christina. Up until the death of Abbot Geoffrey in 1146, Christina's chances of being revered as a saint may have seemed high and a life accordingly begun. Although it was more usual to wait to begin writing until after the death of the candidate for sainthood (not least because of the need to provide a list of posthumous miracles to substantiate the claim), some eager biographers

---

[1] See Rachel Koopmans, 'The Conclusion of Christina of Markyate's *Vita*', *Journal of Ecclesiastical History*, 51 (2000), 663–98.

were known to have been already putting pen to parchment (or at least keeping notes on wax tablets) while their subjects were alive, as, for example, Eadmer in the case of St Anselm and Reginald of Durham for Godric of Finchale. The likelihood of this also happening at Markyate gains plausibility from the strange mixture of sentences in the *Life*, suggesting at one time that Christina is alive and at another dead; there are other indications too that the work was never 'copy-edited', since it contains inconsistencies that would have been unlikely to survive in a polished and completed text ready to accompany any canonization request. What happened to halt the process? It is clear from the *Deeds of the Abbots* that when Geoffrey died, St Albans entered upon a difficult few years, and it may well be that the monks of St Albans at the time, far from being anxious to promote Christina's cult, were all too eager to divest themselves of responsibility towards a woman whom they felt had immoderately preoccupied the abbot, and whose generosity towards her had to their mind recklessly impoverished their abbey.[2]

But what, then, became of Christina? How did she fare after Geoffrey's death? There is no clear answer to this, nor can we even be sure when she died. A gift to her by King Henry II is recorded in the Pipe Roll of 1155, and mention is made of slippers and three mitres she had embroidered being taken as a present to Pope Adrian IV by Robert de Gorron (abbot from 1151 to 1166) on a visit he made to Rome that same year, but neither reference can be taken as certain evidence that Christina was still alive at the time. Nonetheless, if there had indeed been a crisis of confidence in her it seems as if the moment had passed, so that by the mid-century Christina had secured for herself an honourable place in both royal and abbatial circles. All the same, no steps were ever

[2] Ibid.

taken to secure her cult, and we do not even know where she was buried. But her foundation of Markyate survived, a copy of her *Life* was kept there, and before the century was out it had another Christina as its leader. Local memory thus helped ensure Christina's future, but it is the renewed interest, within the last few decades, in women's history and in particular in the contribution of women to the history of monasticism, that has finally brought Christina the fame that Abbot Geoffrey sought for her.

NOTE ON THE TEXT
AND TRANSLATION

THE Latin text used for this edition is that of C. H. Talbot, published as *The Life of Christina of Markyate: A Twelfth-Century Recluse* (1959), with translation, reprinted with addenda and corrigenda in 2002. The *Life* is preserved in a single copy in a manuscript from the fourteenth century, now in London, at the British Library, MS. Cotton Tiberius E. 1. The manuscript was given to the British Museum by Sir Robert Cotton in a damaged state, having suffered in the fire which broke out in his library in 1731. The manuscript is also incomplete, though whether it was ever finished remains a mystery (see Introduction, p. xxiv).

Although we have consulted the manuscript, the task of deciphering any further the charred sections eluded us. Talbot's conjectures, sometimes supplying whole words, sometimes even phrases, have remained our guide. Ellipses remain. We have, however, taken into account corrections to Talbot's text as proposed by P. Grosjean (*Analecta Bollandiana*, 78 (1960), 197–206, at 197–201), and Michael Winterbottom (*Analecta Bollandiana*, 105 (1987), 281–7). Our original intention to provide only a new introduction and notes was overtaken by our realization that the elegance of Talbot's prose at times jeopardized the sense and context of the original. We have tried to keep our revisions in line with modern scholarship, for example, adopting Anglo-Saxon forms of Latinized names (thus Burthred becomes Beorhtred). The text is full of biblical allusions, many representing no more than verbal echoes, some of which are lost in translation. We have included references only to those where the borrowing is substantial, rendering quotations in the King James version. (The numbering of the

Psalms follows the King James version, whereas Talbot cites the different numbering of the Vulgate.)

We are grateful for help and guidance from Santha Bhattacharji, John Blair, David Howlett, Tom Licence, Timea Szell, and Diana Wells.

SELECT BIBLIOGRAPHY

General Background

England

Bartlett, Robert, *England under the Norman and Angevin Kings, 1075–1225* (Oxford, 2000).

Burton, Janet, *Monastic and Religious Orders in Britain, 1000–1300* (Cambridge, 1994).

Clanchy, Michael, *England and its Rulers*, 2nd edn. (Oxford, 1998).

Knowles, David, *The Monastic Order in England* (Cambridge, 1940; 2nd edn. 1963).

Mayr-Harting, Henry, 'Functions of a Twelfth Century Recluse', *History*, 60 (1975), 337–52.

Thomas, Hugh M., *The English and the Normans: Ethnic Assimilation and Identity, 1066–c.1220* (Oxford, 2003).

Warren, Ann K., *Anchorites and Their Patrons in Medieval England* (Berkeley, 1985).

Williams, Ann, *The English and the Norman Conquest* (Woodbridge, 1995).

Yarrow, Simon, *Saints and Their Communities: Miracle Stories in Twelfth-Century England* (Oxford, 2006).

Europe

Bynum, C. W., *Jesus as Mother: Studies in the Spirituality of the High Middle Ages* (Berkeley, 1982).

Constable, Giles, *The Reformation of the Twelfth Century* (Cambridge, 1996).

Hamilton, Bernard, *Religion in the Medieval West* (London, 1986).

Lawrence, C. H., *Medieval Monasticism: Forms of Religious Life in Western Europe in the Middle Ages* (London and New York, 1984; 2nd edn. 1989).

Morse, Ruth, *Truth and Convention in the Middle Ages: Rhetoric, Representation, and Reality* (Cambridge, 1991).

Select Bibliography

Studies in Medieval Marriage

Brooke, Christopher, *The Medieval Idea of Marriage* (Oxford, 1989).

Cartlidge, Neil, *Medieval Marriage: Literary Approaches, 1100–1300* (Woodbridge, 1997).

D'Avray, David, *Medieval Marriage: Symbolism and Society* (Oxford, 2005).

Studies in Women's Monasticism

Coakley, John W., *Women, Men and Spiritual Power: Female Saints and Their Male Hagiographers* (New York, 2006).

Elkins, Sharon, *Holy Women of Twelfth Century England* (Chapel Hill, NC, 1988).

Fanous, Samuel and Leyser, Henrietta, *Christina of Markyate: A Twelfth-Century Holy Woman* (Abingdon and New York, 2005).

Kerr, Berenice M., *Religious Life for Women, c.1100–1350: Fontevraud in England* (Oxford, 1999).

Koopmans, Rachel, 'The Conclusion of Christina of Markyate's Vita', *Journal of Ecclesiastical History*, 51 (2000), 663–98.

Thomson, Sally, *Women Religious: The Founding of English Nunneries after the Norman Conquest* (Oxford, 1991).

Venarde, Bruce L., *Women's Monasticism and Medieval Society: Nunneries in England and France, 890–1215* (Ithaca and London, 1997).

Wogan-Browne, Jocelyn, *Saints Lives & Women's Literary Culture* (Oxford, 2001).

The St Albans Psalter

www.abdn.ac.uk/stalbanspsalter/english/index/shtml (a facsimile with Introduction and Commentary).

Geddes, Jane, *St Albans Psalter: A Book for Christina of Markyate* (London, 2005).

Haney, Kristine, *The St Albans Psalter: An Anglo-Norman Song of Faith* (New York, 2002).

Pächt, Otto, *The Rise of Pictorial Narrative in Twelfth-Century England* (Oxford, 1962).

Select Bibliography

—— Dodwell, C. R., and Wormald, Francis, *The St Albans Psalter (Albani Psalter)*, Studies of the Warburg Institute, 25 (London, 1960).

Powell, Morgan, 'The Visual, the Visionary and her Viewer: Media and Presence in the Psalter of Christina of Markyate (St Albans Psalter)', *Word & Image* 22 (2006), 340–62.

Reference Works

Cross, F. L., and Livingstone, E. A., *The Oxford Dictionary of the Christian Church*, 3rd edn. (Oxford, 1997).

Farmer, D. H., *The Oxford Dictionary of Saints*, 3rd edn. (Oxford, 1992).

Oxford Dictionary of National Biography

Sources in Translation

Matarasso, Pauline, *The Cistercian World: Monastic Writing of the Twelfth Century* (Harmondsworth, 1993).

Morton, Vera, with Wogan-Browne, Jocelyn, *Guidance for Women in Twelfth Century Convents* (Cambridge, 2003).

Petroff, Elizabeth Alvida (ed.), *Medieval Women's Visionary Literature* (New York and Oxford, 1986).

Spearing, Elizabeth (ed.), *Medieval Writings on Female Spirituality* (Harmondsworth, 2002).

Ward, Benedicta, *The Prayers and Meditations of Saint Anselm, with the Proslogion* (Harmondsworth, 1973).

Wogan-Browne, Jocelyn, and Burgess, Glyn S., *Virgin Lives and Holy Deaths: Two Exemplary Biographies for Anglo-Norman Women* (London, 1996).

Further Reading in Oxford World's Classics

Henry of Huntingdon, *The History of the English People 1100–1154*, trans. Diana Greenway.

Jocelyn of Brakelond, *Chronicle of the Abbey of Bury St. Edmunds*, trans. Diana Greenway and Jane Sayers.

CHRONOLOGY

*c.*1096–8   Christina's birth in Huntingdon.

1100   Accession of King Henry I.

*c.*1112   Christina and her family visit St Albans Abbey; Christina takes a vow of virginity.

*c.*1114   Ranulf Flambard, bishop of Durham, attempts to seduce Christina.

*c.*1115   Robert Bloet, bishop of Lincoln, confirms Christina's marriage to Beorhtred.

1116   Christina escapes to a hermitage at Flamstead.

1118   Christina lives with Roger, the hermit at Markyate.

1119   Geoffrey de Gorron elected abbot of St Albans.

1122   Death of Roger the hermit; his burial in the abbey of St Albans; Christina taken under the protection of Thurstan, archbishop of York (through whom her marriage is annulled).

1123   Death of Robert Bloet; Christina returns to Markyate.

1129   Translation of St Alban.

*c.*1131   Christina makes her monastic profession.

1135   Accession of King Stephen.

1139   Outbreak of civil war between Stephen and Matilda (daughter of Henry I).

1145   Consecration of the priory at Markyate.

1146   Death of Abbot Geoffrey.

1154   Accession of King Henry II and of Pope Adrian.

1155   Gift from Henry II to Christina recorded; gifts of her embroidery sent to Adrian IV.

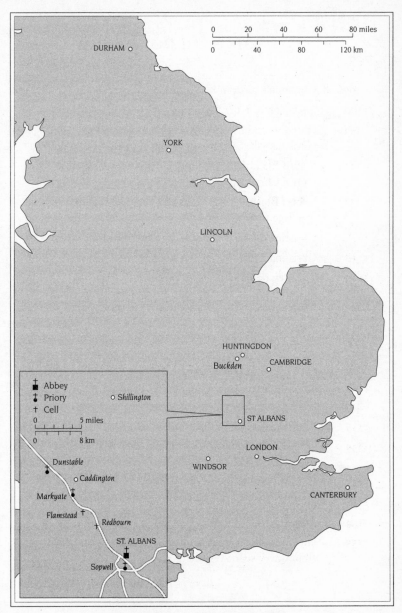

Map of places associated with Christina

THE LIFE OF
CHRISTINA OF MARKYATE

Of S Theodora, Virgin, who is called Christina

A MAIDEN of extraordinary sanctity and beauty was once born to a noble family in the town of Huntingdon. Her father was called Auti, her mother Beatrix.* The name that fell to her in baptism was Theodora,* but later on, out of spiritual kinship, she changed this to Christina. Even before she was born she had already been singled out by God, and this had been revealed to men. While she was still in the womb it so happened that her mother was looking out of her house at the monastery of the Blessed Mother of God that was in the town.* When behold! she saw a dove, whiter than snow, leave the monastery and fly gently straight towards her. With its wings folded, it plunged itself deep into the right-hand sleeve of the tunic she was wearing. Now it was then a Saturday, the day when the faithful pay particular honour to the Mother of God, sometime between the Feast of the Assumption and the Nativity of Our Lady.* Moreover, as the mother herself told me, the dove stayed peacefully with her seven whole days, evidently pleased to be stroked by her hands, nestling happily now in her lap, now in her bosom.

Such a sign was evidently meant to show that the child within her would be filled with that Holy Spirit who appeared above the Lord Jesus in the form of a dove and was described by the prophet Isaiah as being endowed with a sevenfold grace.* It showed also that she would be taught by the example and strengthened by the protection of the Blessed Mary, ever virgin, that she would be holy in mind and body, and that by detaching herself from those things which are of the world she would find peace in the contemplation of things above. As the mother considered these things, she frequently declared that the child she was bearing was such as would be

3

very pleasing to God. And so she carried the child with joy until the day of the expected birth came. Towards daybreak, she went to church, heard matins and the remaining hours, and mass.* She commended herself devoutly and in turn to God, to his Virgin Mother, and to St Leonard,* whose nativity was celebrated that day. After the service she walked back home. Between prime and terce on the same day, that is on 6 November, she gave birth to a daughter, bravely bearing her hour of pain in anticipation of her child. The baby grew and was weaned, and as she grew in body so too did she grow in virtue. Even before she had reached the age of discernment and so did not know the difference between right and wrong, she used to beat her tender flesh with whips whenever she thought she had done something forbidden. Nonetheless she could not yet understand why she should love righteousness and hate iniquity.* In the meantime, since she had heard that Christ was good, beautiful, and everywhere present, she used to talk to him at night and on her bed as if he were a man whom she could see. She did this in a high, piping voice, so that she could be heard and understood by others staying in the same house. She thought that since she was speaking to God, no one else could hear her. But when people teased her, she changed her ways.

At that time there was a certain canon of Huntingdon called Sueno, a man advanced in age, notable for his good life and influential in his teaching. By chance, this man saw Christina when she was still a small girl . . .* For this reason, he was always seeking opportunities (and often found them) of seeing and speaking to her. Both benefited greatly from their conversations. Moreover, as the young girl had decided to preserve her virginity for God, the man of God did all he could to strengthen her in her decision. At times he portrayed the difficulty, at times the glory of virginity: the difficulty in keeping it, the glory in having kept it. On one occasion, when

4

he was speaking about these things, someone said to her: 'This man is still so inflamed by lustful desires that unless he were prevented by the greater power of God he would shamelessly sleep with any deformed and crippled leper.' Christina listened to this with weary contempt and indignantly interrupted, saying: 'If you have anything good to say, speak, and I will listen; if not, I am going.' This reply so strengthened Sueno in the pursuit of holiness that the difference between his former life and the present was as great as that between lead and iron. And in the same way that cement embeds stones in a wall, so too did this biting remark establish him firmly in the love of God. Christina herself made such progress through the teaching and encouragement of Sueno that she considered all earthly goods as but fleeting shadows.

In the meantime, by an act of divine providence Auti and Beatrix took with them their dearest daughter Christina to visit our monastery of the blessed martyr Alban,* where his sacred bones are buried, so as to beseech his protection for themselves and their child. The girl looked at the place intently, and as she thought about the impressive perfection of the monks who lived there, she declared how blessed they were and how she wished to share in their fellowship. When at last her parents were set to leave the monastery, for they had fulfilled all that they had come to do, Christina scratched the sign of the cross* with one of her fingernails on the door so as to mark that in that monastery in particular she had stowed away her heart's desire. And it should be noted that it was then the feast of the nativity of St Leonard, the very day on which she had first been brought into the light of this world. Christina and her parents came next to a village called Shillington,* where they spent the night. Whilst the rest of the party together amused themselves in various foolish ways, the virgin of Christ spent her time alone in holy meditation. Finally, as if it were already the future, she reached the point of imagining herself to be lying on her deathbed, and it struck her that once life departed from the body, no one could foresee where the spirit, now freed, would go. Of one thing, however, she was certain, that if she lived well it would enjoy bliss, but if wickedly, it would be given over to torment. Thereafter she shrank from all the pomp of the world, and turning to God with her whole heart she said: 'Lord, all my desire is before thee, and my groaning is not hid from thee.* Whom have I in heaven besides thee? My flesh and my heart faileth, but God is the strength of my heart and my portion forever. For lo, they that are far from thee shall perish: thou hast destroyed all them that go a-whoring from thee. But it is good for me to draw near to God: I have put my trust in the Lord God, that I may declare all thy works.'* The following day she went to church where the priest was celebrating mass. After the gospel, Christina approached the altar and offered a penny, saying in her heart: 'O Lord God, merciful and all-powerful, receive my oblation through the hand of thy priest. For to thee in surrender of myself I offer this penny.* Deign to grant me, I beseech thee, purity and inviolable virginity whereby I may renew the image of thy Son. Who lives and reigns with thee in the unity of the Holy Spirit, God for ever and ever, Amen.'

After she had returned to Huntingdon, she revealed to her Sueno* what she had vowed and he, considered in those parts as a beacon of God, confirmed the virgin's vow before God. Christina henceforth remained in her father's house in peace, rejoicing that she could grow from day to day in holy virtue and in the love of those things which are above. However, the devil in his envy was unable to bear this any longer, and burning with desire to confound her, he set in motion the following events. Ranulf,* the bishop of Durham, while he was justiciar of the whole of England, holding the second place after the king but before he became bishop, had taken

Christina's maternal aunt, Ælfgifu, as his concubine and had children by her. Afterwards he gave Ælfgifu in marriage to one of the citizens of Huntingdon, and for her sake he greatly esteemed the rest of her kin. On his way to and from London to Northumbria he always used to stay with her. On one such occasion when he was there, his friend Auti had as usual come with his children to see him. It happened that the bishop gazed intently at Auti's beautiful daughter. Straightaway Satan, that songster of voluptuousness, put into his heart* an evil desire for her. Busily seeking some trick whereby to get her into his clutches, Ranulf had the unsuspecting girl brought into his chamber where he slept at night, a room handsomely decorated with hangings, the only others present with the innocent maiden being members of his retinue. Her father and mother and the others with whom she had come were on their own in the hall, enjoying too much drink. As night fell, the bishop gave a secret sign to his retinue and they went off, leaving their master and Christina, that is to say, the wolf and the lamb, together under the same roof. For shame! The shameless bishop indecently seized the maiden by one of the sleeves of her tunic, and with the mouth which he used to consecrate the holy sacrament he urged her to commit a wicked deed. What was the poor girl to do in such straits? Should she call her parents? They had already gone to bed. To consent was out of the question, but she did not dare to resist him openly for had she done so she would certainly have been overcome by force.

Hear, then, how prudently she acted. She glanced back at the door, and saw that though it was closed it was not bolted. So she said, 'Allow me to fasten the bolt, for even if we do not fear God at least we ought to fear men, lest they should catch us in this act.' He demanded an oath from her that she would not deceive him but that she would do as she said and bolt the door. And she swore to him. And so, being released, she darted out of the room, bolted the door firmly from the outside, and hurried quickly home. This was the beginning of all the calamitous troubles which followed. For that wretch, seeing that he had been made a fool of by a young girl, was eaten up with resentment and counted as worthless all the power he had unless he could avenge the insult he had suffered. But he did not believe there was any other way of gaining his revenge unless he or someone else deflowered Christina, since to preserve her virginity she had not hesitated to spurn even a bishop.

In the meantime Ranulf concealed his designs and set out for London. On his return he came to Huntingdon, bringing with him silken garments and precious trinkets of all kinds. He offered them to the maiden; she gazed at everything with utter contempt. The bishop, a slave first to lust but then to malice, saw that he was himself getting nowhere, so he spoke to a young nobleman named Beorhtred, urging him to ask for Christina's hand in marriage, promising that he would further his request in every way he could. The young man acted as the bishop advised. The bishop meanwhile kept his promise with such malicious persistence that he did not stop until her parents had agreed to hand her over whether she liked it or not and Beorhtred had accepted her as his betrothed. This done, the bishop, priding himself on a glorious victory, went off to Durham, while the maiden stayed behind in sadness in her parents' home. Thereafter, the young man in question came to see her father and mother in order to arrange his betrothal* with the girl whom they had promised should be his wife. When they spoke to her about the preparations for the betrothal ceremony, she would not listen. When they asked the reason she replied, 'I wish to remain chaste, for so I have vowed.' When they heard this, they mocked her rashness. She would not change her resolve, whereupon they tried all the harder to convince her of her foolishness. Brushing aside her concerns, they began to press on with plans for the festivities. Christina would have none of it. They gave her presents and made lavish promises. She refused. They cajoled her. They threatened her. She would not yield. Eventually they coaxed a young woman by the name of Melisen, one of her peers and a close friend, into whispering incessant blandishments in her ears, so that by her insistent chatter she would arouse a desire in the heart of her listener for the dignity and status of matrimony. Later we saw this same woman Melisen wearing the veil in expiation, as I believe, of this heinous act. For indeed she worked indefatigably to corrupt her friend, deriving hope of victory from the proverb, *constant dripping wears away a stone.* Nonetheless she was quite unable to extort one word of consent, even though she spent a whole year trying out stratagems of this kind. But sometime later, on a day when they had gathered together at church, everyone, quite out of the blue, accosted the girl. What more is there to say? I do not know how, all I do know is that with God's consent Christina gave in to this chorus of haranguing voices. And in the same hour Beorhtred was betrothed to her.

After the betrothal the maiden returned to her parents' home while her bridegroom, although he had residences elsewhere, built her a new and bigger home near his father-in-law. But although she was betrothed Christina had not changed her mind, openly expressing her determination not to be defiled by submitting herself to the carnal embraces of a man. The more her parents became aware of her persistence in this regard, the more they tried to break down her resistance, leaving no method untried: they flattered her; they reproached her; they gave her presents; they made grand promises; they even threatened and punished her. And although her whole household and the rest of her kin together wore themselves out to this end, her father Auti outdid everyone in this regard, while he himself was outclassed by

9

the maiden's mother, as later events will show. After they had harassed and tempted her in many ways, but to no avail, they finally hit on this artful plan. They put her under a strict and rigorous guard and prevented anyone who was religious and God-fearing from talking with her. Conversely, they brought along people given to jesting, boasting, worldly amusement, and those whose evil communications corrupt good manners.* Furthermore, they stopped her from going to the Monastery of the Blessed Mother of God Ever Virgin, because it seemed to them that whenever she paid a visit there, she came back confirmed and strengthened in her resolve. This was very hard for her to bear, and to those who forbade her, she said with great feeling: 'Even though you can block my way to the monastery of my Lady, for certain you will never erase its memory from my heart.' They forbade her access to the chapel, which was most dear to her, and would not allow her to go there. Instead they took her against her will to banquets, where an excellent variety of dishes was served with various kinds of drink, where the alluring melodies of singers were accompanied by the sounds of the zither and the harp, so that by listening to them her strength of mind might be sapped and in this way she might finally be brought to take pleasure in the world. But their wiles were outwitted at all points and served to show all the more her invincible good sense.

See finally how she acted, how she behaved herself at what is called the Gild merchant,* which is one of the merchants' greatest and best-known festivals. One day, a great throng of important people was gathered together there. Auti and Beatrix, as the noblest present, were presiding, and it seemed pleasing to them that their eldest and most worthy daughter, that is to say Christina, should assume the office of cup-bearer to so honourable a gathering. So they commanded her to get up, to lay aside the cloak she had around her, so that with her garments fastened to her sides with bands and her sleeves rolled up her arms, she should courteously offer drinks to the nobility. For indeed they hoped that the compliments paid to her by the onlookers and the accumulation of little sips of wine would break her spirit and prepare her body for the deed of corruption. But Christina, while carrying out their wishes, shielded herself well against both darts. Against the favours of human flattery she fixed in her mind the memory of the Mother of God, and for this purpose she was helped not a little by the hall where the gathering took place, since because of its size it had many open doors. Frequently, Christina had to go past one of these which happened to look out on the monastery of the blessed Mother of God . . . by reciting the Hail Mary . . .* Against the urge of drunkenness, she placed the shield of her burning thirst. Is it any wonder if she was fainting from thirst, since for the whole day she had, as requested, been serving wine-bibbers while she herself had tasted nothing? In the evening, when it was late, she drank a little water and so recovered somewhat both from the heat and from the thirst that had been overcoming her.

Since her parents had been outwitted in these plots they tried something else, and at night they let her betrothed secretly into her bedroom so that, should he find the maiden asleep, he might suddenly violate her. But through that providence to which she had commended herself, she was found dressed and awake, and she welcomed the young man joyfully as if he had been her brother. She sat on the bed with him and strongly encouraged him to live chastely. She recounted to him the example of the saints, narrating to him in detail the story of St Cecilia and her husband Valerian,* telling him how at their death they were worthy to receive crowns of undefiled chastity from the hands of an angel. Not only this, but both they and many others after them had followed the path of martyrdom and thus, being crowned twice by the

Lord, were honoured both in heaven and on earth. 'So let us,' she exhorted him, 'insofar as we can, follow their example so that we may become their companions in eternal glory. For, if we suffer with them we shall also reign with them.* Do not feel shame that I have spurned you. So that your friends do not taunt you with having been rejected by me, I will go to your house and we will live there for a while ostensibly as husband and wife but in reality living chastely in the sight of the Lord. But first, let us join hands in agreement that neither meanwhile will touch the other unchastely, neither will one look upon the other except with a pure and angelic gaze, promising God that after three or four years, we will receive the religious habit and offer ourselves . . . to whichever monastery providence chooses.' When the greater part of the night had passed in talk of this kind, the young man eventually left the maiden. When those that had got him into the room heard what had happened they joined together in calling him a spineless and useless fellow. With many reproaches they goaded him on again, and on another night thrust him forcefully into the bridal chamber, warning him neither to be misled by Christina's deceitful tricks and naive words nor to let her unman him. He was to get his way either by force or entreaty, and if neither of these sufficed, he was to know that they were standing by to help him. He must just remember to act the man.

When Christina sensed this, she hastily sprang out of bed and, clinging with both hands to the nail that was fixed to the wall, she hung trembling between the wall and the curtain. Beorhtred meanwhile approached the bed. Not finding what he had hoped, he gave the signal to those waiting by the door. They immediately burst into the room, and with lights in their hands ran here and there looking for her, all the more eagerly since they were sure she had been in the room when he entered it and that she could not escape without them seeing her. What, I ask you, do you suppose were her feelings at that moment? How she trembled in fear of her life as they noisily sought her! Was she not faint with fear? She imagined herself already dragged out in their midst with them all surrounding her, leering at her, threatening her, abandoned to the violation of her seducer. Finally, one of them by chance touched and held her foot as she hung there, but since the curtain between them deadened his sense of touch, he let it go, not knowing what it was. Then the handmaid of Christ, recovering her courage, prayed to God saying, 'Let them be turned backward that desire my hurt,'* and immediately they departed in confusion, and from that hour she was safe.

Nevertheless, the next day Beorhtred came back in a similar state of agitated fury. However, as he came in one door she fled through another. In front of her was a kind of fence which, because of its height and the sharp spikes on top of it, was calculated to prevent anyone from climbing over it. Behind her, almost on her heels, was the young man, who at any moment might catch hold of her. With amazing ease she jumped over the fence, and looking back in safety from the other side she saw her pursuer standing there unable to get across. She said, 'Truly in escaping him I have escaped the devil whom I saw last night.' For she had seen in her sleep a devil of horrible appearance, with blackened teeth, which had tried to seize her but in vain, since in her flight she had jumped in one leap over a high fence. While her parents were setting these and many such traps for her, they fixed the day of her wedding. For they hoped that an occasion would arise when she might be caught. For what woman do you suppose could avoid so many snares? And yet with Christ guarding the vow his spouse had made, the wedding celebrations stalled. Indeed, when the day approached which they had fixed, and all the necessary wedding preparations had been made, it happened first that everything which had been got

ready was consumed by an unexpected fire, and then that
the bride herself was seized with fever. And in order to drive
away the fever, sometimes they thrust her into cold water, at
other times they made her far too hot.

Meanwhile, news of Christina's nuptials reached the ears
of Master Sueno, the canon mentioned above. But since a
harsh and severe custody had been imposed on Christina,
Sueno was not permitted to visit her or to receive any message from her. Thinking that she had changed her mind
about her vow of virginity, he accused her of feminine incon-
stancy, saying, 'Truly, to no other . . . since she in whom I put
all my trust deceived me.' This was then relayed to Christina,
namely that her only friend had become her enemy and that,
filled with remorse, he reproached himself for ever having
been her friend and counsellor. When she heard this, she was
struck with profound grief and sat quite rigid and still for so
long that you would have thought she was not a living
person but an image carved in marble. Heaving deep sighs,
she broke out into floods of tears. Sobs punctuated her
laments, as over and over again she bewailed her lot as the
most wretched of orphans. For indeed, despised and afflicted
as she was by her parents and friends, Sueno alone had given
her comfort. His friendly intimacy and sympathy had been
such a source of strength for her that she considered what she
suffered from others as of little consequence. But now, while
the young woman stood firm, the man had faltered; unexpectedly, she was now abandoned and on her own in the
midst of her enemies. Sueno had turned his back on her. But
did Christ desert the one who placed her trust in him? No!
He looked with pity on the lowliness of his handmaiden.*
Turning to him after a little while, Christina said: 'Lord, how
are they increased that trouble me.* Many are they that rise
up against me. I have looked for some to take pity, but there
was none, and for comforters, but I found none.* Unto thee

O Lord do I lift up my soul,* to thee who hast said to thy followers: Blessed are ye when men shall hate you: and when they shall separate you from their company and shall reproach you, and cast out your name as evil for the Son of Man's sake. Rejoice ye in that day and leap for joy: for behold your reward is great in heaven.* I believed that he would be the source of righteousness to me, but in the day of trial I have been forsaken, truly loving thee, following thee, bearing reproaches for thee, enduring the persecutions of men and in thee placing all my trust. For the more a person is despised by men, the more precious he is in thy sight.' Saying this, she was strengthened by the Holy Spirit, and went on with full confidence. There is no doubt that from this moment she was worthy to be signed by the name of her Creator, in that thereafter she was called Christina* even though her baptismal name was Theodora. Indeed, just as Christ was rejected by the Jews, and afterwards denied by the prince of the apostles, Peter, who loved him more than the rest, and was made obedient to his Father even unto death,* so this maiden was tormented first by her parents, then abandoned by her only friend, Sueno. As a follower of Christ, she strove tirelessly to fulfil his will.

In these circumstances, while her parents were oppressing the servant of Christ and growing more and more furious with her, the truth of the matter was made known to Sueno. Reflecting on the constancy of the blessed maiden, and recalling at the same time his own lack of loyalty, the miserable fellow broke out into laments, and beating his breast with his fists, he became the harsh and unmerciful avenger of his own mistake. He sought anxiously to speak with the friend whom he had injured, but because of the watchfulness of her guard he was unable to find any opportunity. However, at last he heard that she was coming with her parents to the aforementioned church of the Mother of God for the purpose of burying some noble kinsman who had recently died. And this I believe was arranged through the cunning of Sueno. When he found the opportunity he sent secretly once, twice, and a third time begging her for the love of Christ not to spurn conversation with a miserable old man from whom she might with good reason turn away because of his lack of trust . . . Raising his hand and putting it to his face, and weeping so copiously that a river of tears washed over his hand, he called God as his witness that he repented of this deed more than any other. Thereby he obtained pardon for his error and renewed his former friendship with Christina. Both of them being happier at this turn of events, the old man remained behind in his monastery, while the maiden walked back home with her parents.

Her father Auti took her back there another time, and placing her before Fredebert, the reverend prior, and the rest of the canons of the house, he addressed them in doleful tones, saying, 'I know my fathers, I know, and bear witness before my daughter that her mother and I forced her when she was unwilling into this marriage pact and that it was against her will that she undertook the oath. Yet no matter how she was led into it, if she resists our authority and rejects it, we shall be made the laughing-stock of our neighbours, a source of mockery and derision to those round about. Wherefore I beg you, ask her to have pity on us: let her marry in the Lord* and take away our shame. Why does she act in this wayward fashion? Why should she bring this dishonour to her parents? Her life of poverty will bring notable disgrace to the entire nobility. Let her now do what we wish and she can have everything that we possess.' When Auti had said this, Fredebert asked him to leave the assembly, and then in the presence of his canons he began to address the maiden in this way: 'We marvel, Theodora, at your obstinacy, or rather we should say your madness. We know that you have been betrothed

according to ecclesiastical custom. We know that the sacrament of marriage, which has been sanctioned by divine law,
cannot be dissolved, because what God has joined together,
no man should put asunder. For this a man will leave his
father and mother and cleave to his wife. And they shall be
two in one flesh.* And the Apostle says: let the husband ren-
der unto the wife due benevolence and likewise also the wife
unto the husband. The woman has not power over her own
body, but the husband: and likewise the husband has not power
over his own body, but the wife. Unto the married I command, yet not I, but the Lord, let not the wife depart from
her husband, and let not the husband put away the wife.*
And we know the commandment given to children: obey
your parents and show them respect. These two commandments about observing the marriage vow and about obedience
to parents are of great importance, and much commended in
the Old and New Testaments.* Yet the bond of marriage is
so much more important than the authority of parents that
were they to order you to break off the marriage, you should
in no way listen to them. Now, however, that they order you
to do something which we know on divine authority to be
more important than obedience itself, and you do not listen
to them, you are doubly at fault. Nor should you think that
only virgins are saved, for while many virgins perish many
mothers of families are saved,* as we well know. And since
this is so, nothing remains except that you should accept
our advice and reasoned doctrine and submit yourself to the
lawful embraces of the man to whom you have been legally
betrothed.'

To these exhortations Christina replied, 'I do not know the
passages of Scriptures you have quoted but I will reply to
you, my Lord Prior, in accordance with their meaning. My
father and mother, as you have heard, bear witness that this
sacrament, as you call it, was forced on me against my will.

For I have never been a wife and have never thought of becoming one. Know that from my infancy I have chosen chastity and vowed to Christ that I would remain a virgin, and this I did before witnesses, but even had they not been present God would be witness throughout to my conscience. This, as far as it was in my power to do, I showed by my actions. You, who are supposed to excel in the knowledge of Scripture, must judge how wicked a thing this would be, should my parents order me to enter into a marriage I never wanted and to cheat on Christ, given that they knew of the vow I had made in my childhood. If I do all that I can to fulfil the vow I made to Christ, I will not be disobeying my parents against the will of God. What I do, I do on the invitation of him whose voice, as you say, is heard in the gospel, "Every one who leaves house or brothers or sisters or father or mother or wife or children or possessions for my name's sake shall receive a hundredfold and possess eternal life."* Nor do I think that it is only virgins who will be saved. But I say, as do you, and it is true, that if many virgins perish so all the more do married women. And if many mothers of families are saved, as you likewise say, and it is true, certainly virgins are saved more easily.'

Fredebert, taken aback by Christina's replies and by her wisdom, asked her: 'How can you prove to me that you are doing this for the love of Christ? Perhaps you are rejecting marriage with Beorhtred in order to enter into a more wealthy one.'

'A more wealthy one certainly,' she replied, 'for who is richer than Christ?'

Then he said, 'I am not joking. I am being serious with you. And if you wish us to believe you, take an oath in our presence that, were you betrothed to him as you have been to Beorhtred, you would not marry even the king's son.'

At these words the maiden, casting up her eyes to heaven, replied with a joyful expression, 'I will not merely take the oath but I am prepared to prove it by carrying red hot irons in these my bare hands.* For, as I have frequently said, I must fulfil the vow, which through the inspiration of his grace I made to the only son of the eternal King, and with the help of this same grace I mean to fulfil it. And I trust to God that the time is not far off when it will become clear that I have no other in view but Christ.'

Fredebert then called in Auti and said to him, 'We have tried our best to bend your daughter to your will but we have made no headway. However, we know that our bishop Robert will be coming soon to his estate at Buckden,* near this town. Reason demands that the whole question should be laid before him. When he is here let the case be put into his hands and at least let her accept the verdict of the bishop as final. Why eat your heart out and suffer in vain? We respect the resolution of this virgin, since it is based on unassailable integrity.'

To which Auti replied, 'I accept your advice. I beg you to ask the bishop to look into this affair.' Fredebert agreed, and so Auti brought back his daughter and placed her again under the usual supervision.

In the meantime, Fredebert heard that the bishop had come to Buckden. Immediately, as sent by Auti, he sought him out, and with him went many of the noblest citizens of the town. All thought that since the marriage had already been performed, the bishop would immediately order the betrothed woman to submit to the authority of her husband. Without hesitation they laid before him in detail everything they knew about the current problem, namely what Christina had done, and what others had done to her, starting from her childhood and bringing it up to the present day. Finally they suggested . . . that since neither adversity nor prosperity could bring her to it, at least episcopal authority should force her to accept her marriage. But after weighing the evidence in every particular, the bishop said, 'I bear witness before you and swear before

God and his blessed mother that there is no bishop under heaven who could force her into marriage if she wishes, according to her vow, to preserve herself for God and to serve him freely rather than any other man.'

On receiving this unwelcome answer, Fredebert and his party returned in some perplexity and reported the bishop's reply to Auti. When he heard it he lost all hope. Full of self-pity, but more to be pitied, he said to Christina, 'Well, we have peace today since you are made mistress over me. By his praises the bishop has exalted you above us all and pronounced you freer than ever. So come and go as I do and live your life as you please, but don't expect any comfort or help from me.'

After saying this, he was each day eaten up by grief. When they saw this, Robert the dean* and certain others took pity on the unfortunate man. They put their heads together to see how they could assuage his grief, and whispered in his ear a plan to compel his daughter to marry, saying: 'Do you want to know why the bishop gave that decision the other day contrary to what was so foolishly asked of him? If you had given him money you would certainly have won your case. Are you not aware of his greed and his lewd nature? Either of these would be sufficient. Imagine the effect of both! His greed will teach him to pervert justice and his lust to envy the chastity of others. Whenever he has any expectation that his friends will give him gifts, he unreservedly takes their side. Do what it takes to win him over and there will be no one to oppose you in future. And so that you achieve what you want more easily, don't hesitate to make use of us as your advocates.' At this Auti recovered hope and put all his cares into their hands. How astonishing is the shamelessness of man, able so to despise the power of God and to rise up against it. But there were in particular two reasons for this, which it may be worthwhile to give here. For once anyone understands them, he will have no difficulty in believing that parents can behave in this way against their own flesh and blood.

One reason was this family's characteristic of pursuing to the bitter end anything it had begun, whether it was good or bad, except where success was impossible. While to persevere in good is counted a virtue, to persevere in evil is the work of wickedness. The other reason was this: such integrity, such beauty, such graciousness shone forth in Christina that all who knew her esteemed her to be above all other women. Furthermore, she was so shrewd in understanding, so prudent in affairs, so efficient in carrying out her plans that if she had wished to devote herself to things of this world she could have enriched and ennobled not only herself but also all her relatives. To this was added the fact that they hoped that she would give birth to children who would take after their mother. So keen were they on these rewards that they begrudged her a life of virginity. For if she remained chaste for the love of Christ, they feared that they would lose her and all that they could hope to gain through her. They did not know how to see beyond worldly possessions, thinking that anyone lacking these and seeking only the unseen would certainly be lost. In the event, everything, as we saw, turned out quite differently. Christina deserted the world and dedicated herself entirely to Christ her Lord as his bride, fulfilling her resolution. Her parents, on the other hand, were subsequently deserted by the world, and fled to her whom they had turned out and took refuge with her, recovering with her both salvation of their souls and the safety of their bodies. Christina thus subverted her parents' expectations . . .

But let us take up the story again. While Auti was secretly and busily discussing with his friends how to approach the bishop, Christina was wondering what these stealthy meetings might mean; I do not know what in particular she suspected, but as is the way with women she was afraid of everything.

In the meantime, as she wondered how she could counter any plots they might make against her, it occurred to her that she could forestall them by blocking the avenue that she thought they were most likely to take. She sent two people of great authority, namely Sueno the canon and her father's chaplain, to her husband to ask him to release her. Among other things, she reminded him of the bishop's pronouncement and begged him not to strive in vain against her since so great an authority had absolved her. These two added their own persuasive words to Christina's message, and Beorhtred, encouraged by the bishop's example, replied, 'If you, who stands in Christ's place, say that my wife does not seek this out of contempt for me in order to marry another man, but so as to fulfil her vow to Christ, then I am indeed ready to release her before God and you. And I will make generous provision* for her out of my own pocket, so that if she wishes to enter into a monastery, she can do so and can be admitted by the community without any difficulty.'

They said to him, 'You speak wisely and in accordance with true doctrine. And lest you doubt the maiden's promise, accept us as guarantors of her undefiled virginity. For the moment, keep your property to yourself, but if you truly do release your wife, even though she is not here, do so now to us, just as if she were present.' And he did so. When Christina's parents heard this they were inflamed with unbelievable fury. They heaped insults on the petitioners of her release and on the instigator, swearing that such an agreement could not and should not stand, because it had been made without their authority. They forced Beorhtred, though not without a great deal of trouble, to feel sorry for what he had done. After this they sent him, harassed by scolding and unsettled by flattery, with the dean and the others mentioned above to the bishop. By saying little but by giving him large bribes they bent the bishop's mind to their will. Christina meanwhile knew nothing about this.

Some time later, on the bishop's orders, Beorhtred and the maiden appeared before him. While Beorhtred was pleading his case against her, the bishop said, 'Take counsel, Christina.'

But she, not knowing that he had been bribed, and putting her reliance on his earlier verdict said, 'Whose counsel can be better for me than God's and yours, most holy father?'

'That's right,' said the bishop, and handed her over to the plaintiff. And she was taken back to her father's house.

As Beorhtred sat beside her, scoffing at her and boasting that he'd bettered her before two bishops, namely of Durham and Lincoln, and had no intention of bringing her before a third, she prayed and said, 'How I wish this last judgement were as true as the first one was false.* For how can you boast you have got the better of me, since with the help of God I have never been yours and never shall be even were I to be cut to pieces. Tell me, Beorhtred, and may God have mercy on you, if another were to come and take me away from you and marry me, what would you do?'

He replied, 'I wouldn't put up with it for a moment as long as I lived. I would kill him with my own hands if there were no other way of keeping you.'

To this she replied, 'Beware then of wanting to take to yourself the Bride of Christ, lest in his anger he slay you.' When she had said this she rose to go away. As she got up, Beorhtred seized hold of her cloak to keep her back; as she moved off, she loosened it at the neck and, leaving it, like another Joseph,* in his hand, she quickly escaped into an inner room.

Now her father became furiously angry. He stripped her of all her clothes except her undershirt, and seizing from her the keys that he had placed in her keeping, he decided to expel her thus from the house. Now Auti was very rich in gold and silver, and he used to entrust into Christina's care whatever precious things he had. In great rage and with the keys in his hand, he said to the girl, stripped as she was of her bodily garments, but more blessedly clad with the jewels of virtue, 'Get out as fast as you can. If you want to have Christ, then naked go and follow Christ.'* And he would have driven her away that very night had there had not been a guest staying with them at that time who interceded for her. For her part, Christina would have chosen to be sent out naked and at night had she been able in this way to have won her freedom to serve Christ, and when morning came she left the house without anyone preventing her. But as soon as her father found out, he quickly sent after her and against her will brought her back. From that day forward her mother Beatrix, with God's permission but at the instigation of the devil, gave free rein to her fury against her own daughter, neglecting no form of evil that she thought might harm her integrity. Even before this she had been most harsh to her, but from then on she persecuted her with unheard-of cruelty, sometimes openly, sometimes secretly. In the end she swore that she would not care who deflowered her daughter, provided that in some way this could be arranged. Thereafter, she wasted a great deal of money on old crones who tried, using love potions and charms, to drive Christina out of her mind with lewd desires. But their most elaborate concoctions had no effect. Finally a Jewess came, intent on harming Christina with particularly powerful magic. She entered Auti's house; she saw the maiden walking by; she said to Beatrix her mother, 'We have laboured in vain. I can see two apparitions, two people dressed in white who accompany the maiden at all times and defend her on every side from all assaults. It is better for you to give up now rather than to strive further in vain.' But Beatrix remained obstinately and maliciously set on her purpose. As she could not score a victory over her daughter, she tried to gain satisfaction from the shameful sufferings she inflicted on her. There was one time when, on an impulse, she took her away from a banquet and, out of sight, seized her by the hair and beat her till she grew tired of it. She then brought her back, lacerated as she was, into the presence of the revellers for them to mock her. The scars on her back never faded as long as she lived.

In such straits, Christ wished to comfort his faithful bride, and gave her consolation through his Virgin Mother. One night, while Christina was sleeping, it seemed to her that she was brought with some other women into a very beautiful sanctuary. And behold: there stood at the altar a certain man dressed in priestly vestments as if ready to celebrate mass. He looked back and intimated to Christina that she should come towards him. As she approached, trembling, he held out a branch of the most beautiful leaves and magnificent flowers, saying, 'Take these, beloved, and offer them to the lady.'

At that moment, he pointed out to her a certain lady sitting like an empress on a dais not far from the altar. She genuflected to her and held out the branch she had received. The lady took it from Christina's hand, broke off a sprig, and gave it back to Christina, saying, 'Take special care of this for me.' Then she added as a question, 'How is it with you?'

And she said, 'Badly, my lady. They hold me up to ridicule and straiten me from all sides. From morning till night I cannot restrain my crying and sobbing.'

'Do not be afraid,' the lady said. 'Go now since I will deliver you from their hands,* and bring you to the brightness of day.'

So Christina withdrew, full of joy as it seemed to her, carrying the little flowering branch in her right hand. And behold: at the place where she had to go down, there was Beorhtred, lying prostrate on the floor, with his face turned to the ground, swathed in a black cape. When he saw her passing by, he stretched out his hand towards her in order to seize and hold on to her. But Christina gathered her garments about her (they were flowing garments of a dazzling white), and clasping them close to her side, she passed by him untouched. As she escaped Beorhtred followed her with his wild eyes, groaning horribly, all the while repeatedly banging his head on the ground in a rage.

Meanwhile, the maiden looked closely in front of her and saw what looked like a lofty, peaceful upper room. It could be reached only by climbing up a series of steep and difficult steps. Christina greatly desired to climb them; while she was hesitating because of the difficulty, the queen whom she had seen a short time before suddenly appeared and helped her, so up she went into the room. And as she was sitting there, delighting in the place, behold! the queen entered and, as if wanting to rest, placed her head in Christina's lap but with her face turned away. This turning away of her face somewhat troubled Christina. She did not dare speak, but in her heart she said, 'Oh, if only I were allowed to gaze upon your face.'

And immediately the empress turned her face towards her and said, with warm friendliness, 'You may look now, and later I shall bring you into my bedchamber together with Judith,* where you may have your fill of contemplation.'

After this vision Christina awoke and found her pillow wet with many tears, and she thought that as the tears she had dreamed were real, so there was no reason to doubt whatever else she had seen in her dream. From that moment you could see that she was a changed person. The immense joy that filled her at the thought of her freedom was evident for all to see in the cheerfulness of her expression.*

Meanwhile, she saw and found an opportunity of speaking with Sueno, the sharer of her secrets, not being able to withhold from him this new source of gladness. She told him in detail of the vision. In turn, Sueno told it to his prior Fredebert. Fredebert, summoning Auti, said to him, 'Take my advice and do not struggle against the judgement of God. Do not cause Christina further pain but respect her as the betrothed of Christ, because if what I have heard is true those who try to harm her or forcibly obstruct her are labouring in vain.' And he told him why.

When Auti heard this he was more disturbed than ever, and his whole household with him. But having once been aroused to anger they were not prepared, as explained above, on any account to desist. When Christina realized this the virgin of virgins appeared once more to her; it happened in this way. The handmaid of Christ saw herself standing quietly by, when quite unexpectedly the Queen of Heaven stood before her. And as she was admiring the beauty of her face and looking at her with great affection, she said to Christina, 'Why do you marvel at me so? I am the very greatest of women. Do you want to know how great? As I stand here it is easy for me to touch the highest point of heaven. And be assured that I have chosen you from your father's house and not only you but also your companion.' And she named a certain man who after his conversion became a most diligent monk in our monastery. I will be quiet about his name since I was ordered so to do.

Sueno, who was unable to find any remedy for the obstinacy of the men mentioned above, importuned Christ night and day for the afflicted maiden's deliverance. At last his prayers and tears were heeded, for one day, when standing at the altar to celebrate mass, there came a voice which said to him, 'Fear not, Sueno, I will set free the woman for whom you have prayed. And when she is free you will see her with your own eyes and speak to her with your own lips and your heart will rejoice.' After this the voice was silent. In the meantime Christ's chosen maiden was spared nothing; far from it, for every day increasingly rigorous measures were taken to prevent her from gaining her liberty. Yet behold! the time was not far off when the divine promise would be fulfilled and the greatness of Christina's prudence and fortitude would be revealed.

There lived in the district a certain man named Eadwine, a devout follower of the solitary life. Christina longed to talk to him so she might have the benefit of his advice. The only way she could do this was by bribing her keepers, which she did, and by their leave, and somewhat apprehensively, she got a message sent to the man. Secretly he came to see her. They seized the opportunity, and as time and place allowed, spoke to each other briefly. She sought advice about her escape; he promised help. When the conversation was over he went away and the event was cleverly hushed up. As Eadwine turned over a number of places in his mind, time and again his thoughts settled on a relative of his by the name of Roger.* This Roger was at that time an old man, mature in wisdom, a deacon in holy orders, a monk by profession, and by virtue of his holy life considered the equal of the fathers of old. He was a monk of ours, but lived in a hermitage, though even here he kept obedience to his abbot. The position of the hermitage where he lived was near the road on the right as you go from our monastery towards Dunstable. Our Roger had been given this place through divine generosity, having been led there by the ministry of angels. For when he was returning from Jerusalem, he had been met at Windsor by three angels clothed in white vestments and stoles, each bearing in his hand a cross over which there were the same number of burning tapers. From there they walked with him, and he could see them all the way, until they had brought him to the site of the hermitage mentioned above where they established him. He later endured much that was terrible in that place, but divine consolation greatly sustained him and allowed him to laugh all this to scorn, since he dwelt faithfully in the commandments of the Lord. No one can ever have suffered more violent temptations from the devil or had more snares laid for him. But armed with the power of the cross of Christ, he overcame the first and avoided the second. Who could have been crueller to his own flesh? He allowed himself no pleasure. With all his might he strove to please God more and more. His compassion on the afflicted and their wretchedness was such that he could not have borne their miseries more keenly had they been inflicted on himself. We have written thus briefly about our old man, by way of introduction, because we think it relevant to our story. The rest we pass over in silence, both because it is difficult to describe and because it is unnecessary to tell here. I refer to Roger's prophetic spirit and powers of contemplation, for which he was famous beyond words.

This old man, then, was straightaway visited by his cousin Eadwine (whom we mentioned above). Eadwine asked him to take the maiden of Christ under his protection since he himself dared not do so on account of her parents. For Christina did indeed come from a family of ancient and influential English nobles, and the whole of that district of Huntingdon for miles around was full of her relatives. When the man of God heard that Christina was from Huntingdon, he carefully asked about her, wanting to know more about her character and her whole story. For he had long been expecting to see something come to him from Huntingdon, but what it was to be, he did not know. Eadwine clearly unfolded the entire story. The old man listened to it all intently. But when Eadwine told him that she had been married, Roger straightaway turned his glaring eyes upon him and finally let out a growl, saying, 'Have you come here to give me a lesson in how to dissolve marriages? Get out of here as fast as you can, and think yourself lucky if you get away unscathed; you deserve a whipping.' And he threw him out of his cell. Since so great a man was horrified at the thought of the separation of a married couple, Eadwine had no idea what to do next. He began to despair and perhaps to regret his undertaking. And he would have returned from whence he came without doing any more, had not the thought occurred to him of going to the archbishop of Canterbury for advice in this difficulty. At that time the archbishop was Ralph,* a man deeply versed both in divine and civil law, as befits a person in his position, and loved by all for his piety.

Eadwine therefore set out for Canterbury, resolved to carry out in every respect whatever the venerable father should decide. He arrived there, asked for an audience with the archbishop, and was admitted into his presence. The others who were there withdrew and the hermit was left alone with the archbishop. Step by step he told him about the life of Christina, how from childhood she had vowed her virginity to Christ and what her parents had done because of this. Nor did he pass over in silence her marriage, but fully recalled with what trickery she had been led into it and by what force. Finally he revealed her desire to escape and asked whether such a plan could be allowed. The archbishop questioned him about the maiden's integrity; the hermit replied that she was inviolate in both mind and body. Then, as a true servant of God, the archbishop grieved over the virgin's trials and afflictions, but gave thanks to God for her perseverance as a staunch soldier of Christ. And he said to Eadwine, 'Believe me, brother, suppose that accursed woman, by whose wiles the virgin of whom we are speaking was seduced into marrying, were to come to me for confession, I would impose upon her the same penance as if she had committed manslaughter. But the blessed virgin made to marry in this way I would without a moment's hesitation absolve. Indeed, I absolve her now, and as the deputy of Christ the high priest who gave me that power, I give her my blessing. Hence I now exhort her to persevere in her vow of virginity, and I pray God that he will bring to fulfilment that angelic desire which he himself inspired in her. But you, my son Eadwine, must not delay: hurry away from here and sustain the precious dove of God with as much help and advice as you can, and may the Lord be with you both.'

Eadwine departed joyfully; he spoke with anchorites at various places on his return and made his way to Huntingdon. On his arrival he found Auti and his wife and their children in the monastery of our Blessed Lady. Christina was among them, but with everyone keeping an eagle-eye on her. This meant that although she saw her ally, she could not speak to him. She did not dare give anyone the slightest hint that she had seen him, even though she had such a desire to know what had been decided on her behalf on the journey. I later heard her say that, had she been given the choice at that moment of either speaking with Eadwine or of having a lump of gold as big as the monastery in which she was sitting, she would without a moment's hesitation have cast aside the gold. She came home sadly with her parents, and on the next day went to her sister Matilda to ask her to get Eadwine to come to her, but she got nowhere. However, she did obtain permission, through bribery, to say a few words to the man's servant. This servant had travelled with Eadwine and knew what his master had done. On hearing from him that there were many places open to her as refuges and hiding-places, Christina chose Flamstead because it was near Roger the hermit, whose servants often visited an anchorite nearby named Ælfwynn, a woman much loved by Roger for her holiness. While he was speaking with her, the servant said, 'How I wish I could keep guard of you outside the town.' At these words Christina was afraid and taken aback, not only because it would be beneath her dignity as a daughter of Auti to be seen in the open countryside with such a youth, but also because it would be very difficult to escape the vigilance of her keepers.

However, she accepted his evident willingness to help her and gave him these instructions: 'Go and tell your master to prepare two horses, one for me and one for you on the day in question,' and she fixed the day of the week. 'When dawn breaks wait for me with the horses in that field, the one over there.' And she pointed to the spot with her finger. 'And I will come down to you there. Don't make a mistake and run up to someone else instead of me. Once my horse is ready, you can recognize me by this sign. I will place my right hand on my forehead with only my forefinger raised. When you see this, rein in the horses immediately. But if I am delayed, take it that I am waiting for the right moment. For my father and my mother will, as usual, be going that day to speak with master Guido.' Guido lived in solitude about six miles away from the town. Bearing all these things in mind, the servant went back and reported them to his master. He was pleased. He got ready the horses and everything else that was necessary.

The longed-for day arrived. After her parents had gone to the hermitage, Christina went out toward the river, carefully scanning the meadow to see if her accomplice was there. As he was nowhere to be seen, she put it down to his laziness and off she went to the church of our Lady the Virgin to receive Sueno's permission to depart. She did not find him there, so without waiting she did the other things for which she had come, that is, she prayed to God that her companion would come soon and that the journey she was about to undertake would be successful. Then she went to her aunt's house. Christina had won her aunt over by giving her presents so that not only would she not betray her niece, she was even ready to help her escape. So with her aunt seemingly watching over her, she spent that day wandering here and there wherever she liked, free from the vigilance of others. At her aunt's house she complained about the late coming of her companion; her aunt soothed and consoled her. In vain, she kept her eyes fixed on the meadow beyond the river. Fearing the return of her parents at any minute, she went out once again to the church of the Blessed Mary. On the way she met the reeve* of the town accompanied by some citizens. He took her by her mantle and entreated her to tell him whether she wanted to run away. She smiled and said, 'I would like to.'

And he said, 'When?'

And she said, 'Today.' The reeve let her go, she entered the church, and falling on her face prayed with great sorrow in her heart, 'Oh Lord my God, my only hope, the searcher-out of hearts and feelings, whom alone I wish to please, is it thy pleasure that I should be deprived of my wish? If thou deliver me not this day, I shall be left in the world, anxious about worldly things and how to please my husband.* My one desire, as thou knowest, is to please thee alone and to be united to thee for all time without end. But whether this be thy decision will become clear if today thou drive me from my father's house and from my relatives, nevermore to return. For it is better for me never to leave it than to return like a dog to its vomit.* But thou seest what is more profitable for me: I wish not my will but thine to come to pass forever. Blessed be thy name for evermore.' When she had said this, she rose and left the church.

Once more she scanned the meadow beyond the river, and when she did not see the man for whom she longed, she turned her steps homeward and sat down amongst her mother's servants, sad at heart and worn out with disappointment. She was already beginning to lose hope, when suddenly something inside her, like a small bird full of life and joy, struck every fibre of her being with its fluttering. She felt it flying upwards towards her throat and forming these words: 'Theodora, arise! Why are you so slow? Look, Loric is here!' (For this was the boy's name.) She trembled, astonished at this unusual voice, and looked around to see if those who were sitting with her had heard it. When she saw they were all busy with their tasks, she immediately jumped up, full of trust in the Lord. Secretly she took the men's garments she had got ready beforehand so as to disguise herself, and set out swathed from head to foot in a long cloak. When her sister Matilda saw her hurrying out, for she recognized her from her clothes, she followed her. Christina noticed this and pretended that she was going to the church of our Blessed Lady. But as she walked one of the sleeves of the man's garment she was hiding beneath her cloak fell to the ground, whether by accident or on purpose I do not know. When Matilda saw it she said, 'What is this, Theodora, that you are trailing on the ground?'

Christina replied with an innocent look, 'Sister dear, take it with you when you go back to the house, for it is getting in my way.' And she entrusted her with a silk garment and her father's keys, saying, 'Take these too, dear one, so that if our father returns in the meantime and wants to take something from the chest he will not become angry on not finding the keys.' When she had allayed Matilda's suspicions with these words, Christina set off as if she were going towards the monastery, but then turned her steps towards the meadow.

Christina made herself known by raising her finger to her forehead, and so found her companion and the horses he had got ready. She seized one of them, but then hesitated, overcome with embarrassment. Why delay, oh fugitive? Why respect your femininity? Put on manly courage and mount the horse like a man. So she put aside her fears, and jumped on the horse as if she were a man, set spurs to its flanks, and said to the servant, 'Follow me at a distance, for I fear that if you ride with me and we are caught, that they will kill you.'

It was about nine in the morning; at about three in the afternoon they reached Flamstead; they had covered over thirty miles in that time. Christina was joyfully welcomed by the venerable recluse Ælfwynn, and on that same day she who had been used to wearing silk dresses and luxurious furs in her father's house now put on a rough garment as her religious habit. Hidden out of sight in a very uncomfortable chamber, hardly large enough on account of its narrowness to house her, Christina was to remain carefully concealed for a long time, finding joy in Christ. On her very first day, she took five verses from the thirty-seventh psalm for her reading, of which the first runs: 'Lord, all my desire is before thee.' A fit passage indeed, and one well suited to the circumstances of the reader. She often repeated it, at times lamenting her own weakness and blindness, at times the violence and guile of her parents, relatives, and friends, who were seeking her life.* But above all, she prayed to the Lord to deliver her from them all, so that without fear she might serve him in holiness and righteousness in his sight all the days of her life.*

In the meantime, her parents had returned from the hermitage, and when they could not find their daughter at home nor among the anchorites of Huntingdon* nor at the monastery of the Blessed Mary, they realized without a doubt that she had run away. But they had no idea where she might have gone. So they sent out search-parties along all the roads that led to Huntingdon with orders to pursue her swiftly, to catch her, to bring her home disgraced, and to kill anyone whom they might find in her company. While some of them went off in a great fury in one direction and others in another, her husband Beorhtred, suspecting that she had found protection with Roger the hermit, went there himself, made careful enquiries from one of his disciples as to whether he knew of any woman there, and offered him two shillings to betray her.

He replied with indignation, 'Who do you think you are, expecting to find a woman here at this hour? It is with the greatest difficulty that a woman is allowed here even in broad daylight and accompanied. And you are looking for some slip of a girl before daybreak?'

When Beorhtred heard this, he hurried off to Flamstead to speak with the venerable Ælfwynn, where he got this answer: 'Stop it, my son! Stop imagining that she is here with us. It is not our custom to give shelter to wives who are running away from their husbands.' Beorhtred, thus deluded, went away, determined never to take on such a mission again.

On the same day, at about three in the afternoon, Roger was sitting as usual at his table about to take his meal when his servant said to him: 'That fellow who came here today before dawn hoping to find a girl didn't know you very well.'

'Who was it?' Roger asked.

'I don't know,' the servant replied, 'but he came from Huntingdon and was looking for some girl of noble family who, so he told me, had run away from her father and her husband.'

On hearing this, Roger heaved a sigh, ordered the table to be cleared and went fasting into his chapel, where night and day, giving himself up to lamentations and tears, he neither ate nor drank until, worn out with sorrow, he sank onto his bed and said, 'I know, O Lord almighty and most rigorous judge, that thou wilt claim her soul at my hands. For I indeed knew that she had noble intentions but I was unwilling to give her my help when she asked for it, and now someone introduced onto the scene at the devil's prompting has abducted her and ruined her while she was off her guard.' As he could find no rest until he found out what happened to Christina, he prayed ceaselessly to the Lord to give him some sign.

After some days, one of his household named Wulfwine set out as he often did to converse with the venerable Ælfwynn. On learning from her about the arrival and concealment of Christina, he went back and told his master Roger. When he heard the story, Roger broke into joyful thanks to the Lord and said to Wulfwine: 'This day, you have called me back from the dead. May the Lord who made heaven and earth be blessed out of Zion.'*

Moreover, when Sueno the canon found out about Christina's departure, he mightily cursed the mother for having driven out the girl for whose sake God had blessed her house. 'You should know,' he said, 'that many dreadful things lie in store for your house, in particular a terrible fire.' All subsequently happened as the man of God had said it would.

Meanwhile it was reported to Ælfwynn, and through her to Christina, that the young man who had helped her to escape was being searched for by her parents so that they might punish or even kill him. All her friends began to grieve at this and prayed to the Lord for his safety. And behold, one night, while Christina was barely awake, the youth stood by her side with a shining countenance and reproached her for her empty fears about those who were seeking her, and encouraged her to put all her trust in the Lord her protector. Next morning, as she revealed the vision to her guardian Ælfwynn and declared that she would be safe, a young man came to say that the youth had been released from the chains of the flesh in a happy death, according to the manner of the faithful. They knew therefore that he who had appeared to her in such a handsome guise, and had advised her to trust in God and to fear nothing from men, was now sharing the company of the elect.

Nonetheless Christina now had another vision by which she was consoled. She saw herself standing on firm ground before a large and swampy meadow full of bulls with threatening horns and glaring eyes. And as they tried to lift their hooves from the swampy ground to attack her and tear her to pieces, their hooves were held fast so that they could not move. While she was gazing with astonishment at this sight she heard a voice saying, 'If you take a firm stand in the place where you are you will have no cause to fear the ferocity of those beasts. But if you retreat one step, at that very moment you will fall into their power.' She woke up and interpreted the place as meaning her resolution to remain a virgin: the bulls were devils and wicked men. Her confidence was thereby strengthened, she conceived an even deeper desire for holiness, and became less afraid of the threats of her persecutors.

In the meantime, her concealment and her peaceful existence irritated the devil: her reading and singing of the psalms by day and night were a torment to him. For though in her hiding place she was hidden from men, she could never escape the notice of demons. In order to terrify the holy maiden of Christ, toads invaded her prison to distract her by all kinds of ugliness. Their sudden appearance, with their big and terrible eyes, was most frightening, for they squatted here and there, settling themselves right in the middle of the Psalter which lay open on the lap of the Bride of Christ for her use at all hours. When she refused to move and would not give up singing her psalms, they went away, which makes one think they really were devils, especially as they appeared unexpectedly, and since her cell was closed and locked on all sides it was impossible to see where they came from, nor how they got in or out.

After Christina had spent two years at Flamstead, the time came when she had to go elsewhere. While she was preparing to leave, Roger's companions, Leofric and his friend Acio, were reciting their offices when they heard a sound, as of virgins singing. They marvelled at the sound and, enchanted by it, rather than singing antiphonally as was their custom, they sang the same verse in unison. At the end of the verse they kept silent and heard the response of the next verse mellifluously sung. In this way, several times, a whole psalm was sung through to the end by the men and the virgins. The men were troubled as to what this could mean, but afterwards it was in part revealed to Roger as he was praying. He immediately called Acio and Leofric to him and said: 'Prepare yourselves and be sure that you are found worthy of the visitation of God, for I am certain that God will soon visit this place, sending us something which he loves greatly. I confess that I do not know what it might be, but I do know that it is something perhaps dearer to God than us sinners.'

A few days later, while Roger was recalling the difficulties that Christina suffered at Flamstead, not only with patience but also with joy, and judging from these and her other qualities that she was deeply rooted and grounded in the love of God,* he decided that he would no longer deny her his protection. And so, in spite of Ælfwynn's opposition, he arranged for her to come and live near him. All the same, he refused to see Christina face to face and spoke to her only through Acio so that there might be no excuse for Ælfwynn to accuse him before the bishop of being a cause of dissension. However, they saw each other the same day, and it happened in this way. The virgin of God lay prostrate in the old man's chapel with her face turned to the ground. The man of God stepped over her, with his face averted in order not to see her. But as he passed by he looked back in order to see how modestly the handmaid of Christ had composed herself for prayer, as this was one of the things which he thought those who pray ought to observe. Yet at the same moment she glanced upwards to appraise the bearing and deportment of the old man, for in these she considered that some trace of his great holiness was apparent. And so they saw each other, not by design and yet not by chance, but, as afterwards became clear, by the divine will. For if they had not had a glimpse of each other, neither would have presumed to live with the other in the confined space of that cell. They would not have dwelt together; they would not have been stimulated by such heavenly desire, nor would such a lofty place in heaven have been kept for them. For the fire which had been kindled by the spirit of God and which burned in each one of them cast its sparks into their hearts by the grace of that mutual glance; and so, made one in heart and soul* in chastity and charity in Christ, they were not afraid to dwell together under the same roof.

Furthermore, through their dwelling together and encouraging each other to strive after higher things their holy affection grew day by day, like a large flame springing from two burning brands joined together. The more ardently they yearned to contemplate the beauty of the Creator, the more happily they reign now with him in supreme glory. And so their great progress emboldened them to live together. Yet they acted with circumspection in not letting this become known, for they feared scandal to their inferiors and the fury of the adversaries of the handmaid of Christ. Near the chapel of the old man, and joined to his dwelling, was a room set at an angle to it. This had a plank of wood set before it, and it was so concealed that to anyone looking from outside it would seem that no one could possibly be inside, since the place was no bigger than a span-and-a-half.* In this prison, therefore, Roger placed his exultant companion. In front of the door he rolled a wooden log, which was so heavy that the recluse herself could not put it in place or remove it. And so, confined in this manner, the handmaid of Christ sat on a hard stone until Roger's death, that is, for four years and more, hidden even from those who were living together with Roger. O what trials she had to bear of cold and heat, hunger and thirst, daily fasting! Even the covering needed when she was cold could not be fitted in, given the narrowness of the place. The place was so well sealed, that when Christina became hot there was no hope of a breath of air. Through long fasting her insides contracted and dried up. There was a time when her burning thirst caused little clots of blood to bubble up from her nostrils. Most unbearable of all was the fact that she was not allowed to go out until evening to satisfy the demands of nature. Even when she was in dire need she could not open the door herself, and Roger usually did not come till late. All she could do was to sit quite still where she was, to suffer in agony, and to keep quiet, because if she wanted Roger to come, she had to summon him either by calling out or by knocking. But how could she do this from her hiding place when she hardly dared to breathe? For she was afraid that someone other than Roger might be near, and hearing her breathing would discover her hiding place; and she would rather have died in the cell than have made her presence known to anyone at that time.

She suffered these and many other discomforts for a long time, and was afflicted by a number of ailments; from day to day these got so much worse that they became incurable. Yet she, for whom no human medicine could bring relief, was, as we saw many years later, cured by an unheard-of grace from God. She bore all these daily anxieties and troubles with the calm sweetness of divine love; she prayed earnestly in those moments at night when she was free to devote herself to prayer and contemplative meditation, just as God's friend Roger had trained her, first by word, then by example. Indeed, he taught her things about heavenly secrets that are hardly credible and acted as if he were on earth only in his body, while his whole mind was fixed on heaven. Some may believe that what I say is false, unless I add a proof to confirm it. She of whom I write, and who was the old man's companion, told me that once when he was rapt in prayer his concentration was so intense that the devil, invisibly incensed, visibly set fire to the cowl that clung to his back as he prayed, and even so could not distract him. How intense then must have been the fire that burned inwardly in his spirit, since it made his body insensible to the actual fire that burned without? It should be believed, therefore, that Christina was no less on fire when she stood by the side of the man in prayer. Not a day passed without his taking her into his chapel for this purpose. How many tears of heavenly desire did they shed! On what rare delicacies of inward joy did they feast!

At first they were haunted by the fear—and it was a deep one, and it spoilt their joy—that if by chance Christina were found in his company she might be snatched away on the orders of the bishop and handed over to her husband to do with as he liked; for the old enemy did not stop importuning these two, and any others he could associate with them, to discover where she was. Therefore she prayed often for Christ's mercy on this matter. And not in vain. For on the day of our Lord's annunciation,* while Christina was sitting on her hard stone giving anxious thoughts to the senseless behaviour of her persecutors, the fairest of the children of men came to her through the locked door, bearing in his right hand a cross of gold. At his appearance the maiden was terrified, but he comforted her with these words, 'Fear not. For I have not come to increase your fears but to bring you reassurance. Take this cross therefore and hold it firmly, slanting it neither to the right or the left. Always hold it straight, pointing upwards: and remember that I was the first to bear the same cross. All who wish to travel to Jerusalem must carry this cross.'*

Having said this, he held out the cross to her, promising that after a short time he would take it back again. And then he vanished from her sight. When Christina told all this to Roger, the man of God, he understood its meaning and began to weep with joy, saying, 'Blessed be God, who sustains his humble servants at all times.' And in English he said to the maiden, 'Rejoice with me, myn sunendaege dohter,'* that is, my Sunday daughter, because just as much as Sunday excels the other days of the week in dignity so he loved Christina more than all the others whom he had begotten or nursed in Christ. 'Rejoice with me,' he said, 'for by the grace of God your trials will soon be at an end. For the meaning is this: the cross which you have received as a pledge will soon be taken away from you.' And it happened just as the man of God foretold.

Two days later, that is, on 27 March, the day on which the Redeemer of the world rose from the dead,* Beorhtred came to Roger's cell with his two brothers, one a canon, the other a layman, humbly asking that he grant him pardon. For he knew and confessed that he had gravely vexed him, and even more Theodora, the handmaid of Christ. He came now to release her from her marriage vows and to submit himself to the guidance and authority of the old man. So, he declared, had it been enjoined on him by Mary, Mother of God, Empress of the World, who two nights before had appeared to him in a terrifying vision, harshly reproving him for his needless persecution of the sacred maiden. Roger, considering that the people who had come with him had little public standing, wisely offered and obtained a breathing-space so that he himself could think over the matter more carefully and Beorhtred could produce other witnesses. At the end of this time Beorhtred returned and released his wife as he had been instructed. Placing his right hand in the right hand of Roger, he promised and confirmed her release in the presence of the following priests: Beorhtred who had married them, Robert dean of Huntingdon, Robert of Flamstead, and before five of Roger's fellow hermits.

After this the man of God felt on safer ground and, full of a confidence engendered by the many virtues he had proved that Christina possessed, he began to wonder about making her the successor to his hermitage. At times he talked to her about this, and though she feared that this would be beyond her capacities, she did not at once refuse but nor did she consent. She acted as she always did, placing both this and her whole future in the hands of the Lord and the Virgin Mary. Whereupon a wonderful thing, more wonderful than any wonder ever, happened. For once, when she was at prayer, and intoxicated with tears in her longing for heaven she was suddenly rapt above the clouds even to heaven, where she saw the Queen of Heaven seated upon a throne and gleaming angels seated about her. Their brightness exceeded that of the sun by as much as the radiance of the sun exceeds that of

the stars. Yet in turn the light of the angels could not be com-
pared to that light which surrounded the Lady who had given
birth to the Most High. It was so much brighter than the rest
that it is hard for you to imagine how her face shone! Yet as
Christina gazed first at the angels and then at the mistress of
the angels, by some marvellous power she was better able to
look through the splendour that encompassed the mistress,
rather than through that which shone about the angels, even
though the weakness of human sight finds brighter things
harder to bear. She saw the Virgin's countenance more clearly,
therefore, than that of the angels. And the more intently she
gazed upon her beauty, the more the sight delighted her and
filled her with joy, whereupon the Queen turned to one of the
angels standing by and said, 'Ask Christina what she wants,
because I will give her whatever it is.'

Now Christina was standing quite close to the Queen and
clearly heard her speaking to the angel. Falling towards the
ground, she saw in a flash the whole wide world. And most
clearly of all she saw Roger's cell and chapel shining bril-
liantly beneath her. And she said, 'How I wish that place
could be given to me.'

And the Empress replied, 'Indeed it shall be given to her
and more, gladly, should she want it.'

From then on she therefore knew that she would be
Roger's heir. Roger, in consequence, was anxious before God
and men to provide her with a patron who would take care of
all her needs. At length Archbishop Thurstan of York* came
to mind, for he was a helpful supporter of such vocations,
so Roger sent to him to ask what he thought could be done
for Christina. Thurstan asked to have a private conversation
with her. In some urgency, the old man sent for Godescalc
of Caddington* and his wife, people very close to his heart
and of good family, who lived exemplary married lives under
his direction. He told them in confidence how and why he

wanted them to take Christina to Redbourn.* When they had agreed to the undertaking and been given leave to depart, Roger the man of God said to them, 'Go with all confidence because I shall pray for you and you will perhaps not regret the trouble which you are taking for God and his handmaid.'

So they set off, mounted on only one horse. As the beast was labouring up a steep incline through woody paths, the girths broke and the saddle fell to the ground with the riders on it. What were they to do? It was night. The horse had run away. They had no one with them and they were beginning to feel their age. Even had it been daylight, they would not have been able to catch up with it. Finally, leaving the saddle where it was since they could not carry it, they set off on foot, groping their way in the darkness as best as they could. But as they grew weary, sadness overcame them and they said, 'Where is God's promise?' The words were hardly out of their mouths when a horse, saddled and bridled, stood beside them, quiet as a lamb, near a fallen tree trunk which seemed as if it had been put there on purpose to help the servants of God mount. When they saw it they gave thanks to God and his servant Roger and, mounting the beast, they set off home.

Next morning Godescalc went back to Roger, took Christina from him, and brought her secretly to the archbishop at Redbourn. The archbishop talked privately with her for a long time, and on learning from her what was necessary he took her from that moment into his keeping.* He promised—and later fulfilled the promise—that he would see to the annulment of her marriage, to a confirmation of her vow, and for permission for her husband to marry another woman by apostolic indult.* Then he sent her back home.

Christina remained then with Roger in his hermitage up until the time of his death. When he had gone to heaven, where he rested in certain peace after his many hardships, it became essential for Christina to go elsewhere to avoid the anger of the bishop of Lincoln. After she had attempted to hide in various places, the archbishop finally commended her to the charge of a cleric, a close friend of his, whose name I am under obligation not to divulge. He was at once a religious man and a man of position in the world. And relying on this twofold status, Christina felt particularly safe in staying with him. And certainly at the beginning they had no feelings for each other, except chaste and spiritual affection. But the devil, the enemy of chastity, could not for long bear this situation. And he took advantage of their close companionship and feeling of security to infiltrate himself stealthily and with guile, then later on, alas, to assault them more openly. And, loosing fiery darts, he pressed his attacks so vigorously that he completely overcame the man's resistance. But the devil could not wrest consent from the maiden, even though he titillated her flesh and put ideas in her head. He used the person she was staying with to set traps and play many evil tricks on her. Sometimes the wretched man was so aroused that he came before her naked, burning with lust and quite beside himself, and behaved in such a shocking way that I cannot make it known lest by such shamefulness I pollute the wax* by writing about it or the air by saying it. Sometimes falling on the ground, he implored and beseeched her to have pity upon him and to have compassion on his wretched state. But as he lay there she upbraided him for showing so little respect for his calling, and she dismissed his advances with harsh reproaches. And though she herself was struggling with this wretched passion, she wisely pretended that she was untouched by it. Whence he sometimes said she was more like a man than a woman, where she with her masculine qualities, might more justifiably have called him a woman.

Would you like to know how manfully she behaved when she was in such great danger? By long fasting, little food and only raw herbs at that, a ration of drink, sleepless nights, and harsh scourgings she vehemently resisted the desires of her own flesh, lest her own members become the agents of wickedness against her. And what was more effective than all of these . . . the trials which tore and tamed her lascivious body. She called upon God without ceasing not to allow one who had taken a vow of virginity and had despised the marriage bed to perish for ever. Only one thing brought her respite: the presence of her patron. For then, her passion cooled; for in his absence she used to be so inwardly inflamed that she thought the clothes which clung to her body might catch fire! Had this happened while she was in his presence, the maiden might well have been unable to keep herself in check. One day, as she was going to the monastery, the devil,* her evil genius, appeared to her in the form of an enormous, ferocious, ugly, shaggy bear, trying to block her way into the monastery. Nothing repelled the arrows of his attack as effectively as the humility of the virgin as she offered her prayers and tears. As she went on her way, the earth swallowed up her despairing foe . . . the virgin escaped from his snares, yet she was ill thereafter for more than a fortnight.

Nonetheless, even though she was quite ill the lewd cleric continued to molest Christina quite as much as he had done when she was well. At last, three saints, John the Evangelist, Benedict the founder of monks,* and Mary Magdalen, appeared to him in his sleep and threatened him. Mary, whom the priest particularly revered, glared at him with piercing eyes and reproached him harshly for his wicked persecution of the chosen spouse of the most high king. At the same time, she threatened him that if he harassed Christina any further, he would not escape the anger of the Almighty nor eternal damnation. Terrified by this vision and wakened from sleep, he went to the maiden in a different frame of mind, revealing to her what he had seen and heard, seeking and receiving pardon for his offences; thereafter he emended his ways. Nevertheless, neither this nor anything else could cool the maiden's passion. So, after a long time spent in constant warfare against her tireless adversary, and finding her lodging deadly and hateful, she returned to the happy place of solitude given to her by the Queen of Heaven and there, day and night, she prostrated herself in prayer. Weeping and lamenting, she begged to be freed from temptation. Even in solitude she unwillingly endured lustful urges. Then the Son of the Virgin looked kindly down upon the lowly estate of his handmaid* and brought her the consolation of an unheard-of grace. In the guise of a small child, he came to the arms of his sorely tested spouse and remained with her a whole day, not only being felt but also seen. The maiden took the child in her hands, gave thanks, and pressed him to her bosom. And with immeasurable delight she held him at one moment to her virginal breast, at another felt him in her innermost being. Who shall describe the abounding sweetness with which the servant was filled by this honour paid her by her creator? From that moment, the fire of lust was so completely extinguished that never after could it be revived. About the same time, the bishop of Lincoln, Christina's most persistent persecutor, died; after suffering long punishment his life was cut short by sudden death, and by his example others were deterred from persecuting the virgins of Christ.

The handmaid of God remained then in her solitude in relative security; embracing the peace she had so long desired, she recalled with what mercy Christ had delivered her from so many dire straits. Astonished at the greatness of the grace she had received, she every day offered a sacrifice of thanksgiving* to her deliverer. This then was her special joy, her one purpose, to spend her time in praising God and in giving thanks. In the meantime, God decided to make known how great was her merit in his sight. In Canterbury lived a certain woman of good family. She was dear to her parents but because of her infirmity, known as the falling sickness* (contracted through her own rash fault when she was already grown up), she had become a nuisance to them and had been cast out. She had endured this sickness for two years, every Tuesday at nine o'clock. In the third year of her misery God sent her the blessed martyr and virgin Margaret,* who in a vision had admonished her to go to God's friend Christina, then living in a hermitage not far from St Albans monastery, and to drink water which she had blessed with her hands in the name of the Trinity. She would then recover her health.

The woman arose without delay and, buoyed up by hope, quickly came to see Christina. She first confessed her fault, then spoke of her wretchedness, and thirdly, told Christina what had been revealed and asked if she could be relieved. Christina refused, saying it had nothing to do with her, that she had not been sent to her but had perhaps been deluded by a dream. The woman boldly persisted with her entreaties and enlisted the help of Ælfwine, the priest, and some others who were present. And though they pleaded with Christina for a long time not to be so obstinate and not to refuse the grace of God which was at hand to help, she would not agree until they had promised that the priest should celebrate mass while the others should join with her in praying for the mercy of God on this matter. This she did to ensure that the grace of recovery should be attributed to their merits, not to hers. On the morning of the Tuesday, therefore, they gathered together in the chapel and all prayed to God while Christina blessed the water and gave it to the woman to drink. And during the canon of the mass,* a handsome figure solemnly clothed, bearing a book in his hands, came towards the woman, stood face to face before her, and opened the book. Christina, who was the only one of those present able to see what had happened, knew that Christ had sent his apostle and had cured the woman. When the office was over, she explained all this to her. Willing to believe but full of doubt, the woman stayed in the chapel, trembling, until nine o'clock. Indeed she stayed there until midday. Then seeing that her hour had passed, she knew for certain that she had been cured. Weeping copiously for joy, she asked them all to give thanks to her redeemer. And on her promising that during the lifetime of Christina she would tell no one how she was cured, they sent her away.

Christina, who obtained cures for others from heaven, herself suffered from grievous ailments which she had contracted through the various trials she had endured. And as time went on new ones were added to the old. And as they were all beyond the reach of medicine (for everything known to human science had been tried in vain), she was cured quite unexpectedly by divine power. But first listen carefully how appropriately Christ cured her of one particular illness, and that the worst, through his mother, and then how wonderfully he cured her of all the rest by sending her a crown from heaven to signify her virginal integrity. The disease, known as a paralysis, attacked one half of her body, spreading from her lower limbs to the top of her head. As a result of a recent illness the cheeks of the sufferer were already swollen and inflamed. Her eyelids were contracted, her eyeball bloodshot, and underneath the eye you could see the skin flickering without stopping, as if there were a little bird lurking inside striking it with its wings. Because of this, experienced doctors were sent to her who to the best of their ability practised their profession with medicines, bloodletting, and other kinds of treatment. But what they thought would bring relief had in fact the opposite effect. Indeed the condition, which they ought to have eased, became so irritated and inflamed that she suffered from it for five whole days without ceasing, so that what her health had been in comparison with her sickness before treatment, now her sickness became in comparison with the illnesses that followed. Moreover, so that no time should be lost in effecting her cure, nor in curtailing her suffering, a certain old man sent her a remedy which, dissolved in wine and drunk, would, or so he claimed, eradicate and expel the disease from her. But in order to ensure that the spouse of God should put her trust only in divine help, her final suffering was as much greater than all the rest as the second was greater than the first. So violent was it on the sixth day that at any moment she was expected to breathe her last. But on the following night, by the will of God (who rested on the seventh day),* she woke up and found herself restored to health and, thanks be to God, to us. For no matter at what hour she was to be released from the prison of her flesh, who could doubt that her spouse would come and lead her with him to his nuptials? She felt a movement of her eyelids, and sight in the eye that had been blind, the swelling seemed gone from her cheeks, and she felt relief also to the lower parts of her body. So surprised was she, she could hardly believe this, so she called her maidens together and corroborated the fact with a lighted candle. On the following day, when everyone had come together, they began to talk about the sudden cure of their mistress.

Then one of them said that in the first watch of the night she had seen, in a dream, a woman of great authority with a shining countenance whose head was veiled with a snow-white coif, adorned across the breadth of it with golden embroidery and fringed on either side with gold, who had sat down before the sickbed and had taken out a small box in which she had brought a remedy of exceptional fragrance. As she was carefully preparing to give it to her, all of those present warned her with tears in their eyes, saying, 'Do not waste both your remedy and your work since we saw the woman you are attempting to cure barely escape death yesterday after taking a similar remedy.' She took no notice of what they were saying and gave the remedy to the sick woman, as intended, whereupon the woman was cured. The patient who was cured and the servant who had seen the dream discussed both cure and vision with all the greater joy, because before their talk the one was unaware of the vision, the other of the restored health. See how easily and how aptly God, through his Virgin Mother, cured his virgin daughter through celestial medicine, judging his spouse unworthy of any mortal cure.

It now remains to reveal how she was released from her many other illnesses, for they were many in number. Each was worse than the paralysis. They threatened to cut short her life, but she had no wish to die until she had been professed. Besides, great men from renowned monasteries, both from distant parts of England and from far across the sea, often visited her, wanting to take her away with them to add importance and lustre to their foundations by her presence. The archbishop of York in particular tried very hard to honour her by making her superior over the virgins whom he had gathered together under his name at York,* or as an alternative to send her over the sea to Marcigny* or at least to Fontevrault.* But she preferred our monastery, both because the body of that notable athlete of Christ Alban rested there (whom she loved more than any of the other martyrs whom she revered) and because there, Roger the hermit had been a monk and was buried.* And as you know by experience, she loved you more than all the other shepherds on earth under Christ; moreover there were certain souls* in our community whom she cherished more than those in other monasteries, some of whom had become monks because of her. And it should be borne in mind that as our most blessed patron, St Alban, asked for her from the Lord as joint labourer in the building up and furthering his community on earth, so afterwards she would become a sharer of his eternal bliss in heaven. For these reasons she decided that she would make her profession in this monastery and would accept the blessing of her longed-for consecration from the bishop, but inwardly she was in a great state of agitation, not knowing what she should do nor what she would say when, at the moment of consecration, he would ask about her virginity. For she remembered the forcefulness of the thoughts and the stings of the flesh with which she had been troubled, and even though she was not aware that she had fallen either in deed or desire, she did not dare assert that she had escaped unscathed from such great storms. At last, she turned with her whole heart to the most chaste Mother of God, pleading with her and asking her that by her intervention she might be relieved of this uncertainty. While she was caught up in these thoughts, she began to feel more confidence about their resolution, which she hoped would happen about the time of the feast of the Assumption of the Mother of God.*. For this reason she had no peace of mind until the feast-day actually arrived. The nearer it grew, the more anxiously did Christina complain about the sense of delay she felt. At last the day came, but her hopes were not immediately filled. The first day passed; the second day passed; so in the same way six days of the festival* passed. However, her prayers never became any the less fervent; indeed, both her devotion and her hope increased as the days went by.

On the seventh day, that is 21 August, before dawn and at about cockcrow, she got up and stood before her bed. The hour had passed at which it was usual to sing nocturns.* She thought this must be due to the laziness of her maidens, and saw that all around they were fast asleep. Moreover, there were none of the accustomed sounds; everything was strangely sunk in a deep silence. The virgin was standing in astonishment when behold! there gathered around her young men of extraordinary beauty. What a remarkable sign of mercy and divine approval! Although there were many present, she could only make out three. These greeted her and said, 'Hail virgin of Christ. The Lord Jesus Christ has commanded that greetings be sent to you.' And when they had said this they drew nearer and, standing round about her, placed the crown they had brought with them on her head, saying, 'This has been sent to you by the son of the most high king. Know that you are one of his own. You marvel at its beauty and craftsmanship but you would not marvel if you knew the art of the craftsman.' It was indeed, as she herself said, whiter than snow and brighter than the sun, of a beauty that could not be described and of a material that could never be known. From the back, and reaching down beyond her waist, hung two white fillets like those of a bishop's mitre. Thus crowned, Christina stood among these angels who had been sent to her from cockcrow until the day grew warm from the rising of the sun. When the angels withdrew into heaven she remained alone, knowing for certain from the heavenly crown that Christ had safeguarded her as a virgin in mind and body. Moreover, she felt in such good health that never after did she feel the slightest twinge from those illnesses which had afflicted her before.

Disturbed by these events, the demon burst forth into new warfare, so regularly terrorizing the friend of Jesus Christ that for many years afterwards, whenever she was exhausted and settled herself down to sleep, she did not dare turn over onto her side in bed nor look about her. For it seemed to her that the devil might stifle her, or by his nefarious arts drag her into some obscene games. But when he was foiled in his unwearying attempts to debauch her mind, the poisonous serpent plotted to break her steadfastness by creating false rumours and spreading abroad unheard-of and incredible slanders through the bitter tongues of his agents. Everyone with a perverse frame of mind, prompted by malice and goaded on by that incorrigible liar, took pleasure in disseminating every imaginable evil about her, each one thinking himself to be the more admired, the more wittingly he fabricated lying tales about Christina. The handmaid of Christ, sustained in the midst of all this by her good conscience, committed herself to the mercy of her redeemer and submitted her case to divine judgement. In order not to depart from the path of our Saviour, she prayed for those who cursed her.* The devil soon realized that whatever darts he threw, Christina would deflect by her shield of faith,* and that because she was possessed of the love of God she could not be seduced by worldly love. The bold and audacious warrior, so that he should leave nothing untried, did not fear to attack the virgin through the spirit of blasphemy.

The devil's own faith taught him that he might be able in some way to darken and stain Christina's faith, and so he attempted to veil and stain the mind of the virgin. He suggested time and again horrific ideas about Christ, detestable notions about his holy mother, but she would not listen. He kept attacking her, but was put to flight. He continued his assaults, but was routed. Even so he would not be silenced. When put to flight, he would not disappear; when routed, he would not retreat. Taking up new and more exquisite weapons of temptations, he attacked the virgin all the more intensely since it pained him so deeply to be beaten by a young virgin. Finding her alone in the chapel, he sometimes molested her with such grotesque apparitions and terrified her with such harsh threats that any other person would easily have been driven mad.

Persecuted by these and other such torments, the handmaid of Christ was inwardly disturbed and feared that God had abandoned her. She did not know what to do nor where to turn nor where to go to avoid the machinations of the devil. At last she collected herself, and strengthened by the memory of previous acts of compassion she went to church, bathed as was usual in tears. She threw herself before the eye of God

and placed herself at his mercy. But when she remembered
that God leaves no sin unpunished, she wondered if by chance
these and many other grievous ills might not have come about
through her own fault. She prostrated herself on the ground
and, raising her mind, she prayed earnestly to Jesus, for she
was afraid that if help did not come soon, she would be
tempted beyond her strength even though God allows no
man to be tempted beyond his strength.* And behold, while
she was prostrate in prayer, with nothing to distract her, and
while she was rapt from earth to heaven, she heard (though in
what way I do not know) these prophetic words: 'Do not be
afraid of these horrible temptations, for the key of your heart
is in my hand and the lock of your mind and body is in my
custody and no one can enter unless I allow it.' Immediately
she felt freed from all anxieties, as if they had never been, and
for the rest of her life, whenever she was assailed by temptation or overwhelmed with sorrow, she remembered the key
and in confirmation of Christ's promise to his handmaid she
would quickly experience heavenly consolation. But the virgin
of Christ was still being tried in the crucible of poverty, lacking those things which by their absence increase rather than
lessen virtue. For her beloved and loving spouse and lord did
not wish to give her a hundredfold reward here for all she had
forsaken, lest earthly affluence cool her spiritual love. She, for
her part, would not receive anything she needed from anyone
unless it was given in a spirit of true love and holy compassion. But when he who knew her secrets thought it appropri-
ate to help her even in these matters, this is how he did it.

In the neighbourhood of that hermitage was a certain noble
and powerful person, versed in both kinds of knowledge:
Abbot Geoffrey of St Albans.* At the beginning of his prelacy
he governed the house committed to him with great rigour
and brought it prosperity. But fortune smiled upon him
through the support of his noble relatives, and this led him to

become more arrogant than was right and to rely more on his own judgement than on that of his monks over whose religious counsels he presided. This man was not yet known to the maiden of Christ except by common repute. She had not made his acquaintance, nor had she ever seen him. Nevertheless, God decided to provide for the needs of his virgin through this man and through her to bring the man back to the fullness of his vocation. And this is how it began. The abbot had at one time decided to carry out a project, which he knew could not be accomplished without causing annoyance to his chapter and without offending God. As a man of considerable determination, it was not easy to deflect him from his purpose. Once embarked on a high-handed course, he often added obstinacy to his determination. However, he had not as yet discussed his proposal with anyone.

Now, there had lived in the monastery of St Albans under the aforesaid abbot a certain man of great probity, known and friendly to the virgin of Christ of whom we are speaking: his name was Alfred, who, being perfected in good things, had not lost his life but changed it. He appeared to Christina, in such a way that she could plainly see him. As befits a friend of light, he carried a brightly burning candle in his hand. He began to speak to Christina in this way: 'The Lord Abbot Geoffrey, without consulting the chapter, has decided on a course of action (and he explained the matter) which is not without moral danger, for if he carries it out he will offend God. The task I ask of you is to prevent him from doing it. This command I bring you from God.' This said, he disappeared. Thinking this over, the virgin began to wonder whether or not to obey the command: 'If I do perhaps the abbot will not listen to me but if I don't, I fear I will incur divine judgement.' The fear of God overcame the fear of man, so she summoned a messenger to tell the abbot what she had seen and heard and she did what she could to persuade him not to carry out his plan. The abbot grew angry, thinking the order nothing but a silly dream, and sent back a message to the effect that the handmaid of Christ was not to put her faith in such nonsense. However, he was astonished that something had been revealed to the virgin which as yet was only taking shape in his mind. When Christina received his insolent reply, she relied as ever on her usual practices of fastings, vigils, and prayers, and pleaded with God that, as she had not been able to dissuade him, someone else should divert the abbot from his course. God did not spurn the prayer of his beloved virgin. What more is there to say? Night came; the aforesaid man (the abbot) had that day decided in his proud obstinacy to carry through his project; now he sought his bed ready to take some rest. But in the first watch of the night he saw many black, terrifying figures standing around him. They launched an attack on him. They threw him out of bed; they struck him, suffocated him, and tortured him in various ways. Beset and tormented on every side, he was about to breathe his last when, turning his gaze, he saw the aforesaid Alfred, his eyes and whole face blazing in anger. At first neither spoke to the other. Plucking up his courage amidst his distress, the abbot said, 'What is it, master, that you order me to do?'

Alfred growled in reply, 'You know very well. You received an order and yet you did not relinquish your wicked plan.'

'Holy Alfred,' he groaned, 'Holy Alfred, have mercy on me. I will give up my evil ways and henceforth I will obey her commands without delay.' At these words Alfred withdrew, the torturers departed, and the torments ceased.

When morning came the abbot felt there was no time for delay, for the scourging had been real enough. He took to one side his closest associates in the monastery, explained the project to them in detail, and promised to put an end to it. They all praised God and extolled the holiness of the virgin. From then on the abbot implicitly complied with the warnings and commands of the virgin. Mindful of his promise, and not unmindful of the beatings, he hurried to visit the hand-maiden of Christ, acknowledging his debt to her for the message and thanking her for his deliverance. He promised to give up everything unlawful, to fulfil her commands, and that he would himself be the patron of her hermitage. All he asked was her intercession with God. These great things were achieved through you, O Christ, who through an outpouring of grace can bring help to your own through whomever you may choose. In this way, your virgin was relieved of anxiety about material concerns, while the abbot through the virgin was freed from spiritual anguish. Thereafter, the man came often to visit the servant of Christ; he heard her admonitions, accepted her advice, consulted her when he was in doubt, drew back from bad decisions, bore her reproaches. Both worldly affairs and pastoral care entailed much work on his part and seemed to him to disturb the peace he greatly desired. In dismay, he went to the handmaid of Christ for advice as if to a place of refuge, and he received her answer as if it were a divine oracle, recalling the words of the Gospel, 'it is not ye that speak, but the Spirit of your Father which speaketh in you'.* If he went disconsolate, he returned consoled; if tired of the ups and downs of the world, he returned revived. He withdrew under the shadow of him whom lovers find,* and when he grew cold in divine love, he rejoiced to find renewed fervour after speaking with her.

The virgin Christina sensed that the abbot was, in his heart, now ready to resume more fruitful tasks. She could see that through the intervention of someone as insignificant as herself he had become eager to overturn many evils and to put in place many good projects, and she therefore cherished him with great affection and loved him with a wonderful but pure love. For she was so filled with the Holy Spirit that she neither knew how nor wanted to love carnally. Their affection was mutual but their sanctity took different forms. Geoffrey supported Christina in worldly matters; she commended him to God more earnestly in her holy prayers. If anything, she took more care for him than she did for herself and watched over his salvation with such attention that, wonderful to relate, the abbot, whether near or far away, could not offend God either in word or deed without her immediately knowing it in the spirit. Nor did she make a secret of reproving him harshly in his presence whenever she knew that in his absence he had gravely sinned, thinking that the wounds of a friend are better than the flattery of an enemy.* This will be made clear from the present example.

Whenever Geoffrey was sorely tempted to sin, he imagined Christina to be present, for he knew that scarcely anything was hidden from her, and so he easily repelled temptation with the strong shield of faith. And as God scourges every son whom he receives,* so he scourged that abbot with a serious illness that brought him to despair for his life. And although he put no trust in man, yet he put great trust in God through man, in other words through the handmaid of God, Christina. One remedy he had left—and it was considerable—and that was to be able to commend himself before death to the virgin herself. So he decided to invite her. Straightaway messengers and horses were got ready to set out on the next day. Nothing of this was hidden from Christina. Barely a day before, one of his fellow monks, an unassuming and God-fearing man, had come to her, saying that she ought to visit the abbot who was ill. And she had said, 'I have learned that one should not carry lilies without reason.' She went into her little chapel and prevailed on God with her prayers and tears to give her, by his grace, a sure indication of the state of the abbot's health, in ways that she could hear and see. . . . For she wore a short, sleeveless tunic whenever she left the enclosure of the hermitage . . . as she was leaving the chapel she . . . the wall and

felt herself carried over a room and she saw him for whom she
had been labouring sitting in a corner there, resting his head
on the staff he had become accustomed to carry because of
his illness . . . monks of the church . . . namely master . . .
Evisandus and two virgins of Christ, Margaret the sister of
Christina,* an admirable virgin of holy integrity, and Ada,
who had sought Margaret out as a companion while she was
visiting her mother (who was staying in Westminster), and
was now returning to see the abbot who seemingly was at
death's door. Christina, aware of all this, was overjoyed to
hear the voice of the abbot, saying, 'How I wish that it would
please our Lord Christ to let my lady Christina know that we
are sitting here together.' The monks and the women joyfully
concurred. Christina came to herself, and after matins prayed
earnestly to the Lord to give quick and merciful relief to the
abbot. Not unmindful of the prayers of his handmaiden, her
holy patron gave back health to the abbot, joy to the community, and saved a faithful servant of the church. As he felt
his strength returning, the venerable man wished the virgin
would come after the office of matins, and though he greatly
wanted to be consoled by the conversation of the virgin, yet
reason prevailed over desire. On the very next morning, at
daybreak, Margaret, whom we have already mentioned, came
to her sister's beloved dwelling-place. After a prayer, having
said *Benedicite*,* as is the custom, and without saying anything else, Christina ordered her sister to be silent and she
related everything to her in detail, how she had seen the abbot,
what she had heard from him, and what those who had been
seated around had said. Margaret acknowledged the truth of
it, marvelled at what had been done, and gave glory to God
who works through his saints. After he had recovered his
health, not unmindful of her kindnesses, the abbot went back
to the virgin whom he so dearly loved, hoping to derive further holy inspiration from her sweet conversation. Nor was

his wish in vain. Margaret came to him and told the abbot everything in detail, how all their words had been revealed to Christina in the spirit and how she had learned everything from her.

Abbot Geoffrey revered the virgin and recognized in her a rare quality of holiness. From that time forward he visited her devotedly, thinking little of the hardship of the journey in comparison with its rewards. Nevertheless, he hardly if ever went to her without her having some spiritual foreknowledge of his coming, and this she would reveal to one of her companions. And since she realized that he was striving with all his might towards higher things, she surrounded him with special care, praying for him with tears almost all the time. In God's presence she would often put him before herself. And as she herself confessed, of all those with whom she shared Christ's fellowship there was no one for whom she was able to plead to God with such devotion and urgent prayer. And so it came about that she often foresaw assaults and snares which demons had prepared; these, by long intercession, she often overthrew and in this way strove to keep her beloved, for this is what she used to call him, in a state of peace.

On the day before Pentecost,* she called together three of the maidens who were living with her (for as Christina's reputation grew so did the number of her maidens). She predicted that on that very day he whom she held dear in her heart would come. She ordered them to tidy up everything, to behave devoutly, lest her monastic friend be offended by anything that displeased him. Believing what she said (for past events gave them confidence), they obeyed the commands of their mistress. The abbot put off coming. For he had decided that he would give no intimation of his visit to anyone, so that then it would be kept a secret. Mass was said. No messenger came from the abbot. The maidens looked at one another in astonishment at the delay. Only one thing was certain,

Christina could not have misled them nor could she have made a mistake. Suddenly a messenger appeared and all rejoiced at the news that the abbot was on his way. The venerable man arrived, and engaged in an uplifting and delightful conversation with the virgin. And while they were talking he said, 'I know that this time, my sudden arrival was kept hidden from you.' But Christina called to her sister Margaret who knew her secrets and the others to whom she had spoken about it, and ordered them to speak out about what they had heard about his visit. And they, obeying the friend of truth, confirmed the truth. Praise to God rose from them all: and the grace of the Holy Spirit was felt all the more abundantly that day.

Christina stayed in that same hermitage for a long time before receiving from the bishop the consecration of her virginal humility and humble virginity. She was advised by many wise and religious persons, and by her close circle and friends, to put her neck under the yoke of obedience and to confirm her vow by solemn consecration, saying that it was fitting that as her vow had made her a spouse of Christ, so she should be marked by a wedding to Christ. She put off the ceremony, uncertain whether she should remain in that place or whether, as she had once thought, she should seek some remote spot, possibly a town off the beaten track where she might enkindle a passion for Christ. At last, inspired by God and persuaded by the frequent pleading and humble sweetness of the abbot mentioned above, she gave her consent to their suggestion. And so on the feast of St Matthew,* who is said to be the first consecrator of virgins, Alexander, bishop of Lincoln,* consecrated the virgin of Christ.

In the fourth year of her profession, about the octave of Epiphany,* the abbot was in great pain and troubled by a fever. In his compassion God arranged to scourge* him by way of a reward, when previously he had scourged him by way of punishment. Christina, the abbot's consoler whenever he was seriously ill, was some distance away. So the abbot sent a message to his proven patron, asking her to come to his help in this hour of need as on previous occasions. Christina went to her usual sanctuary; she threw her body on the ground; her tears flowed. As her heart cried out, the Lord heard her prayers and health was restored to the invalid. Intuitively she already felt the efficacy of her prayers, as a voice came from heaven saying, 'Know for certain that your beloved will come with joy to see you in five days from now.' It was then Sunday. Christina quickly left the chapel and said to the messenger, who was about to leave, 'On your way back, as you are hurrying here, when you reach such and such a place, tell your master from me, "Tomorrow, white stones will be thrown into the pot",' a charming proverb which is quoted when success is assured, as if to say, 'when your master has recovered his health he will hurry to see me'.

But the servant, convinced of his master's ill health, said, 'My Lady, this is impossible. He has such a serious fever and at times feels so shivery, that he can scarcely lie down, let alone ride a horse.'

'Go,' she replied, 'and be confident that he will recover and do what I have told you. But above all, I beg you not to breathe a word of this until you reach the place that I have mentioned.'

The messenger accepted the order, took care not to disobey it, returned, and found his master on the road to recovery but not saying anything about making a journey. He kept secret what he had heard until the outcome was established. Early on the appointed day horses and retinue were prepared for an urgent visit to the virgin. They reached the aforementioned spot and then at last the messenger delivered Christina's words to his master. He was amazed. 'Did the virgin know', he asked, 'that my recovery would be so sudden and that I should make the journey today?'

'She knew,' he replied, 'she made it known with such and such signs.' The wise man, confirming the present from the past, was aware both of the Saviour's mercy and of the maiden's assured care of him.

One Christmas night, at matins, Christina was giving her whole mind to contemplation of the greatness of the birth. In her meditation she became more and more inflamed with desire; at such times the remembrance of her beloved friend often came to her. In some ways she was more anxious for him than she was for herself, and hence a voice came to her saying, 'Would you like to see him for whom you are anxious and how he is?' And when she answered, 'I would', she saw Abbot Geoffrey (for he it is of whom we are speaking) vested in a red cope, his countenance transcending human beauty and glory, not with a simple brightness but with a brightness shimmering with ruddiness. At this sight Christina was deeply reassured, and from that time she became so attached to him that neither favour nor malice could prevent her from calling him her closest friend whenever occasion arose. Nor did this happen without much spiteful gossip. For there were many people who wished to reach the same holiness of life and gain the same affection from Christina as the abbot enjoyed. But falling out of favour, they delighted in slander. After two days, namely on the third day after Christmas, Alexander the sub-prior of the church came to visit her. When he was asked, he replied that the abbot had been vested in a white cope, but the maiden said, 'Think carefully again if that is really true, because on that night I was there and saw him vested in a red cope.'* Alexander recalled, not without astonishment, that this was so and glorified Christ all the more devoutly in Christina. How she saw this vision, though she herself well knew, we were not able to find out from her as long as she was with us.

From then on, the abbot withdrew all his hope from the world and fixed it utterly on Christ. He laboured with all his might at whatever was useful, renouncing from the depths of his heart the things of the earth and longing for those of heaven. One consolation gladdened him, that unknown to the world, he could bestow his earthly riches on the poor of Christ. Indeed, far from seeking unjust gain, he justly lavished his possessions on worthy causes. What he had previously squandered on worldly ostentation now he sought to bestow as unostentatiously as possible on hermits, recluses, and others who were in need, thus deserving the apostle's commendation 'as having nothing and possessing all things'.* All this he attributed to the grace of God and watchful care of the maiden. And he became so changed a man from what he once had been that he who had striven for worldly glory would not now, even for the whole world, offend God in the slightest way. There was one thing above all which he ardently wished to know about the virgin. It was this: by what zeal for purity or what prerogative of virtue was such grace given her that, by the prompting of the spirit, she quickly knew of his deeds whether done secretly or far away? When he spoke of some such, she would reply, 'I know all about it,' and would then tell him in detail what he was going to say. So, giving it much thought and turning it over in his mind, he wondered how he could find out about it. If he went about it lackadaisically he feared negligence, if boldly, rashness. Puzzled by these and similar problems, he passed whole days until evening, and spent many sleepless nights.

One night, however, he saw himself holding a flowering herb in his hands, the juice of which was very efficacious for driving away ailments. Anyone who squeezed it strongly would get little juice out if it, but if gently and lightly, he would get what he wanted. Next morning he hastened to accompany the religious man, Evisandus, to his beloved hermitage. On the way they discussed the dream, coming to the conclusion that the herb was Christina and the flower the honour of her virginity; and he said that she should not be interrogated aggressively but questioned gently and kindly. (And later we often found this to be the case.) The abbot told everything to Christina. For, very early in the morning, after her devotions, she came out of the church and walked in a little enclosure close by that was filled with herbs. She plucked the first she found, which happened to be a *camilla*.* She took it reverently in her hand and went toward the abbot as he approached, as if about to greet him, and said, 'This is the herb, is it not, which you saw in your vision during the night?' And she showed him the plant; for she had learned this in a revelation from a voice above. The abbot and Evisandus marvelled at what they heard; the first recounted his vision, and both told of their conversation along the way, glorifying God who reveals to 'babes what he conceals from the wise and prudent'.* And so the merciful God solved the problems of the investigator and made the beloved virgin more loveable to the abbot.

Another time it happened that her beloved was sitting on his bed before daybreak in a wakeful state, thinking about certain things that would be useful, and as he turned his eyes this way and that he saw clearly—for it was no dream—he saw, I say, that same handmaid of Christ near his head, as if she were anxious to see how he bore himself towards God in his innermost thoughts. He saw her with others he knew, but could not speak to her. But he was overcome with joy and amazement, and the rest of the night passed to his great benefit. When morning came, he rose and asked to see one of his relatives, by the name of Leticia, who was that day going to the virgin's hermitage. For she too was leading the religious life. 'Go,' he said, 'and tell your beloved mistress that her anxiety about me is evident. For truly, as I lay awake I saw her visiting me last night;' and he mentioned the place and the time and the hour. For he thought that Christina knew nothing of it.

When Leticia arrived, she began to deliver the message entrusted to her. But as soon as she opened her mouth, Christina silenced her and sent for the virgin of blessed memory, her sister Margaret (she wished to summon her lest Leticia had her doubts), and ordered her: 'Tell me in Leticia's hearing what I mentioned to you first thing this morning about that dream.'

And Margaret replied, 'My lady, you said that for certain, last night at such a place and hour, his daughter had been to see him' (for out of humility this is what she called herself). 'And you added that if this had happened in the time of blessed Gregory,* he would have preserved the event for posterity, even though it is a small thing. But I replied that it was not small but something marvellous and worthy to be remembered by those who come after us.'

On hearing this, the aforementioned Leticia was greatly edified and glorified God in his saints, saying: 'This is the Lord's doing and it is wonderful in our eyes.'*

From that time on Geoffrey, dedicated to good works, visited the place ever more often. He often benefited from the virgin's conversation, provided for the house, and became its administrator. While he busied himself in supplying the maiden's needs, she strove to enrich the man in virtue, pleading for him with such earnestness to God in prayer and with such concentration that at times she did not notice that he was there. After receiving the Eucharist, or whenever she took part in the celebration of mass (for she communicated at the table of Christ as often as the abbot celebrated the mysteries of the divine word), she was so rapt that, unaware of earthly things, she gave herself to the contemplation of the countenance of her creator. Knowing this, the abbot used to say, 'Great is my glory in this, that though for the moment you are forgetful of me, you present me to him, whose presence is so sweet that you fail to realize that I am present.'

Now the handmaid of Christ, disciplining her spirit by vigils and her body by fasting, stormed God in prayer and would not cease until she was satisfied in her mind that the salvation of her beloved was assured. God listens more attentively to the prayers of the pure, and even before he is invoked says, 'I hear.' This he deigned to show by means of a vision: Christina saw herself in a certain room; it was finely built and it smelt sweet. Two venerable and handsome figures clothed in white garments were present. They stood side by side, differing neither in stature nor beauty. On their shoulders a dove, far more beautiful than any other dove,* seemed to rest. Christina saw the abbot outside, wanting to get in to her but not being able to. Giving her a sign with his eyes and head, he humbly begged her to introduce him to the people standing in the divine presence at her side. The virgin lost no time in coming to her friend's aid with her usual prayers. With all the energy of which was capable, with all the love she could pour out, with all the devotion she knew, she pleaded with the Lord to have mercy on her beloved. Without delay, she saw the dove glide through the room with a fluttering of its wings, feasting the eyes of the onlooker with its sweet gaze. When she saw this, God's devotee was heartened and she did not cease praying until she saw the aforesaid man either possessing the dove or being possessed by it. And when she came to herself she understood more clearly that the dove represented the grace of the Holy Spirit, and that the abbot, once filled with it, would only be satisfied with divine consolation. Filled with joy at this, she cherished and venerated him as a fellow and companion of heavenly rather than of earthly glory, and took him to her bosom in a closer bond of holy affection. For who shall describe the longings, the sighs, the tears they shed as they sat and discussed heavenly matters? Who shall put into words how they despised the transitory, how they yearned for the everlasting? Let this be left to someone else: my task is to describe quite simply the simple life of the virgin.

This same virgin had a brother, Gregory, a monk of St Albans whom she cherished with extraordinary affection on account of the charm of his manners and the staunchness of his belief. In general her relations with her family were far from easy, except in cases where their integrity or their inborn goodness commended them to her. This Gregory then, with his abbot's permission, stayed for a short time with his sister and used to say the Divine Office there. But the day approached on which God had decided to snatch him from the cares of this life, and he was seized with that sickness which was to usher in his final day. His sister had great compassion on him (for at that time she was noted for her love of good men). She resorted to her usual remedy of prayer, and pleaded with God to reveal to her in his mercy what plans he had in mind for her brother. The result of her prayers was long in coming, but their constancy never flagged, even though her brother's flagging health seemed to forebode death. At this Christina grew yet sadder, and for the sake of her brother moved Christ with floods of tears until she heard a voice from above saying these words, 'You may be sure that his Lady loves him.' And after a moment the voice added, 'She loves you also.' Convinced, therefore, of the death of her brother, and also convinced that her own was imminent, she gave thanks to God, both because she had deserved to be heard but more because she had learned that both of them would be summoned by the queen of queens. So going to her brother, she intimated to him that the Queen of Heaven would summon him. And she added, 'If some noble and powerful lady in the world had called you to her service while you were in the world, you would have taken great care to appear pleasing to her. Now that the Queen of Heaven calls you, how much more should you fulfil her commands to the best of your ability while you can!'

When Gregory heard this, believing that his death was near, he fortified himself with the sacraments of Christ in a spirit of composure gained from his sense that he was about to die. After he had received the viaticum* and all those things which concern the burial had been decently arranged, he was borne unconscious to the church in the presence of the abbot and all the community of St Albans, not without the tears of many mourners. Full of hope, he breathed his last. While he was alive he had dearly hoped that both his sisters Christina and Margaret would be present at his burial, as indeed they were.

In the year when Stephen was first elected king of England,* he decided on the advice of wise counsellors to send ambassadors to Pope Innocent II* at Rome in order to obtain from so great a father the confirmation of his election. For the fulfilment of this embassy the first, or among the first, to be chosen was Geoffrey, abbot of St Albans. He was summoned to the king's court to hear the edict. He went quickly to the virgin to commend himself to her holy prayers. He discussed the summons of the king, though as yet he did not know its reason. She, sadder than usual, said, 'Go, go and may the grace of God accompany you. But you should know this journey will not be successful. For I do not feel about you as I am accustomed to in the divine presence.' The visit to the king's court went ahead; the royal decree concerning an embassy was announced; it was not declined. It was an unhappy journey, and the reason for the journey unhappier still. Geoffrey returned home to arrange his expenses for the expedition. Once again, he visited his divine sanctuary and discussed the task imposed on him. He admitted his grief, and in proof shed tears of grief. He asked for two undergarments* from Christina, not for pleasure but to relieve the toil of the task ahead. Nevertheless, he begged her to pray earnestly to God, asking that his will on the matter might be made known.

She went to her beloved hideout, her face suffused with tears, her heart torn with sighs. She continued in prayer day and night, until she heard a voice coming to her from above, 'Behold the wall.' And she saw a wall, in which her beloved friend was, as it were, cemented alive. 'As long' (the voice continued) 'as he is firmly fixed in it, the protection of God will never fail him. But the undergarments which you have prepared for his comfort, give as quickly as you can to the poor, because Christ will obtain greater consolation for him on his journey.' Certain it was a divine promise (for she was not inexperienced in these matters), Christina turned her tears into joys and her sighs into devotion.

Meanwhile, the venerable Thomas,* whom we have mentioned above, whom the abbot had sent to the highest people in the realm to seek his release from the embassy, did not find him with the king but preparing to go to Rome. On returning from the court, he assured the virgin that no reason could be found for postponing her beloved's departure. All agreed that he should undertake what had been ordered. But she said, 'I beg you to have no further anxiety about these matters, for this is what has been told me and this is what I have seen.'

He believed her, for he was well aware of her hidden powers, and exclaimed, 'Why should I not follow him and persuade him to return?'

'That won't be necessary,' replied the virgin, 'he has been relieved of the burden of the journey. But I think it is right that the king's favour should be recompensed with a divine gift.' So in giving away the undergarments, she fulfilled the command, while he, in keeping back her beloved, confirmed the promise. And she counted it little loss to dispose of the woven goods so long as he, whom true charity had woven, was kept back from undertaking so burdensome a task.

In the third year of the reign of the same King Stephen, Pope Innocent II summoned a general council* to Rome.

Apostolic letters ordering this convocation were dispatched everywhere, England included. At that time, the Roman legate,* Bishop Alberic of Ostia, was as of right holding a council. When the papal mandate was received, a general discussion took place as to what should be done. And since it seemed dangerous in times when war was imminent for all the prelates of England to leave the country and make the difficult crossing of the Alps, certain of them (the more prudent) were chosen to undertake an embassy on behalf of themselves and the others. Among those first to be chosen was Abbot Geoffrey. Nor did he much object, for as he was popular in the papal court, he was looking forward to seeing his old friends again. Nevertheless, he wanted to have the virgin's approval of this decision. For he did not believe that Christina would fail to talk to Christ about so great an enterprise. Coming joyfully to her, he told her that he was being sent to Rome on business concerning himself and the realm. He could not refuse, especially as the papal mandate was urgent. As usual, she was slow to reply; only in her heart did she cry out against the plan. At last, checking a sigh, she said, 'Go forth in the Lord, for whether you go or whether you stay, I am certain that the divine will will be fulfilled in you. For when I was at prayer, I saw a certain place surrounded by a shimmering fence; it was transparent and like a cloister without a door or windows, but it was round and the grass inside was greener than ordinary grass. Overjoyed by all this I saw you, the cause of my anxiety, within this enclosure, standing happily enough with an enviable degree of pleasure. And while I was still anxious as to how you would get out, whether by digging or some other way, it was said to me, "God alone is the doorkeeper of this enclosure which you see and that man cannot come out except by divine intervention." Because of this, and strengthened by the mercy of Jesus Christ, I am confident that you are being held in this enclosure and prevented from setting out on your journey.'

While Geoffrey for his part hurried to Oxford, where the king's court was being held, Christina hurried to the eternal king to pray about the same journey. At the king's court and with the earthly king, discussions were held about the abbot's departure. Meanwhile, with God, the celestial king, Christina discussed how the same man might be kept back. She, who knew how to love to supreme advantage, gained the day. She knew how to love in this way because she made it her practice to pray to God in every case for a just outcome. For by divine providence, and contrary to the efforts of many, and the wishes of everyone, letters were sent by the apostolic legate to the archbishop of Canterbury, Theobald,* recalling the abbot. And he who previously had been destined to set out on the journey now joined the others who were to stay behind in discussing who should go. And so Geoffrey realized that the purity of the virgin had more power with God than the factious and shrewd cunning of the great ones of this world.

In the same year, the aforesaid King Stephen, on the advice, albeit wicked, of some of his courtiers, took into his custody two bishops, Roger of Salisbury and Alexander of Lincoln,* because he suspected them of being too powerful in wisdom, castles, wealth, and family connections. He put them in prison, which befitted neither their position nor their ecclesiastical status. On being called to account for this action by Theobald, archbishop of Canterbury, and by some of his suffragans, he gave his word that he would answer to the judgement of the church on the matter of their capture. At the appointed time they met at Winchester. On one side was the king with his barons and their retinues, on the other the archbishop, bishops, and abbots of almost the whole of England, with a concourse of clergy come to discuss such an important matter in the presence of the Roman legate, namely Henry, bishop of Winchester.* The king was cited on his promise to undergo sentence, but he refused on oath to submit to any judgement on these matters unless it were favourable to himself and his party. The king's mercy was requested but not shown; ecclesiastical censure was threatened but despised. What more is there to say? Hostile enemies of the Church strove to sow discord between king and clergy. All of a sudden, the king, thinking that the clever council of certain people of remarkable cunning was outwitting him, felt compelled to appeal to Rome to avoid being struck then and there by the rod of excommunication.* And when both sides had arranged to send representatives to Rome, the aforesaid venerable Abbot Geoffrey was chosen with others to uphold the rights of the Church, since he was judged in the opinion of all as well suited to defending such rights.

What was he to do? To refuse was bad policy, to accept the charge dangerous. For the king had threatened to confiscate the property of all those who went to Rome to contest his will. On the one hand, Geoffrey perceived that in his state of health the task was beyond his strength. On the other, if he undertook the journey he had to consider the cost to the poor, for whose material well-being he had lovingly laboured. There was nonetheless one consolation left to him, and that was well founded: to seek the divine will on these matters. For he did not care to place the glory of this world even in the slightest degree before the divine will. Hastening therefore to his sweet and known remedy, I mean the servant of the Lord Christ, Christina, he explained to her what the orders were and what a decisive moment this was. He begged, pleaded, and implored her, seeing the importance of the case, to intercede with God most earnestly, and moved the already sympathetic virgin with his tears.

The abbot departed certain only of one thing, the burden of the journey. She, deploring the position in which her beloved found himself, but fearing more for the danger to his soul than to his body, invoked him who watches over these matters and for whom she had abandoned everything. Her prayer was as usual prolonged, and as she was rapt in ecstasy she saw herself in the presence of her Saviour. She saw him, whom she loved above all others, encircled with her arms and held closely to her breast. And while she feared that, since a man is stronger than a woman, he would in one way or another be able to extricate himself, she saw Jesus, the helper of the saved, clasping her hand with his own holy hand, not by intertwining his fingers with hers but by joining them one over the other so that, by joining her hands as well as by the power of her arms, she should feel greater strength in holding back her beloved. On perceiving this, she was more than a little overjoyed and gave effusive thanks, both because she knew that her friend was relieved of his trouble and particularly because she was aware of the presence of her spouse and Lord. Within a short time, by the disposition of God's mercy, all those who were being sent abroad heard of their dismissal from this burdensome journey.

After a while the abbot was called again to the court, not knowing what the king wanted. He was, all the same, afraid that cunning, malicious liars might turn the king's heart against him in some way. For the king was sometimes more inclined to believe flatterers than those who spoke the truth. On his way there the abbot turned aside to the virgin to commend himself to her prayers since, when fortified by her, adversities held no terror for him, for he had experienced her help so often and in so many ways. In the midst of their conversation (for they spoke always of the things of God first), the abbot said, 'I am going to the court. I do not know when I will come back for I fear the fickleness of the king.' It was then a Sunday.

'Why are you troubled?' said the virgin. 'Why be concerned when the Almighty is your protector? Go in confidence, for you will find the king's mind well disposed towards you and you will return to me next Thursday in a happy frame of mind.'

Geoffrey set out with joy. He went to the court and everything turned out just as he had hoped. And on the day foretold he joyfully revisited his beloved to thank her. He could not have come before because he had been immersed in business, though he wished that he need not have delayed so long.

There was something wonderful about her, but also awe-inspiring. Often while she was speaking she was rapt in ecstasy, and saw whatever it was the Holy Spirit wished to show her. At such times she neither felt nor knew anything of what went on about her or what was spoken. For when her prayers were heeded she received certain trustworthy signs, on account of which she endeavoured to plead with God more earnestly. Sometimes she saw Evianus* (but not in the flesh) lightly caress her face and mouth with his first and middle finger; at other times she felt a little bird fluttering gently with its wings within her breast. But when her mind roamed more freely, sometimes she saw one, more often three, lights shining with equal brilliance and splendour, so much so that she believed that, had any of her friends been present, she could have shown these same lights to them. Whichever of these signs she saw, it meant that her requests had been heeded. For these visions were not fantasies or borne of dreams; for she truly saw them with the intuition of those deserving spiritual vision. Very often also, when she slept more soundly than usual as a result of long vigils and bodily exhaustion, as soon as the hour for matins approached she awoke so easily that you would scarcely believe that anyone else could have heard a sound. But so zealously did Christ watch over his handmaid that if anyone molested her, they were either swiftly made to do penance or afflicted with some bodily ailment; we heard, for example, about someone who had been stricken with blindness, another who had left this life without the sacrament,*

others who were eaten up with envy and lost all the reputation for holiness they had once enjoyed.

But, Satan, surely your darts were not blunted in the
midst of all this? Surely you were not compelled into corrupting many others just because of Christina and because you
despaired of corrupting her? Surely not! For a depraved and
perverse generation* which accused Christ Jesus of casting
out devils in the name of Beelzebub, which despised the disciples of Christ because they took women about with them,*
that same generation, because it lacked good sense, did not
perceive the good savour of Christ spread about by Christina,
since they could not detect sweet smells, but saw only the
smoke. Driven on by their own malice and urged by the envy
of the devil, they spent their time in pursuing Christina, the
beloved of Christ, with much gossip, poisonous slanders,
barbed words, trying to defame her who had tried so hard to
hide her fame from men. Some called her a dreamer, others a
seducer of souls. Others, less brutal, called her a worldly-wise
business-woman. In other words, what was a gift from God
they attributed to worldly know-how. Others, who did not
know what else to say, spread about the rumour that she was
bound to the abbot by ties of carnal love. In this way, divided
amongst themselves, each one, according to his own devil,
persecuted her, fortified as she was by the protection of Jesus
Christ. To all these there was but one crumb of comfort,
insulting though it was: namely, if they could not deflect the
virgin from her path, at least they could falsely make many
people believe evil about her. And as the good savour of Christ
is life for the good, so the good savour of Christ is death for
the bad. But the savour of Christ* remains good everywhere.
And so it came about that the common folk, who revel in any
gossip, were assailed by rumours. Henceforth the lance of
envy pierced some of those who wore the habit of religion.
Some chattered about things neither true nor remotely so.

Others strove to cover their fictitious tales under the veil of truth, so that listening to them you might think that one was Jerome, the other Paula,* had not one been a virgin and the other the mother of a virgin. Before they had come to love each other in Christ, the abbot's well-known integrity and the virgin's holy chastity had been praised in many parts of England. But when their mutual affection in Christ inspired them to greater good, then the abbot was slandered as a seducer and the maiden as a whore. No wonder. For Zabulus,* their enemy, feared the advantage they could gain one from another and the extent to which they would benefit the Church. He wished to turn the reason behind their extraordinary progress into the cause of their downfall. But all his attempts were turned to his own disadvantage. For many of the people (as we ourselves have seen) who took pleasure in slandering her returned to the path of truth, confessed their fault, and obtained pardon, whilst those who had played the part of the false accusers afterwards became the true advocates of the truth that dwelt within her. God recalled with manifest signs some of those who up to that point were unaware of how things stood and were left in some uncertainty. This can be proved by the following example.

In the monastery of Bermondsey, near the city of London, there was a man venerable in his way of life, a true monk, living up to the meaning of his name Simon,* who was sacristan to that house and who, on account of his holiness and the strictness of his life, was a leading member of that community. This man had great respect for the virgin just mentioned. He relished her company and spoke about her with love, since through the sweetness of her friendship he had felt a greater outpouring of the Holy Spirit. He was so opposed to tale-bearers and detractors that he checked anyone whom he heard at the first word. But as he knew that God should defend just causes, he decided to beg him who is the judge of

79

thoughts and desires and the knower of all secrets to reveal to him the truth about Christina. For this reason he afflicted his body with fasting, his mind with watching and tears; he slept on the hard floor and would accept no consolation until he received some answer from the Lord. For he considered it a crime to make false accusations against Christina, and he would not believe that he had been led astray by his love for Christina. God therefore wished to put an end to his troubles and show the truth to the lover of truth.

One day, when the venerable Simon was standing at the altar celebrating mass, still thinking of his question, he saw to his astonishment Christina standing at the altar. He was amazed: the virgin could not have come out of her cell; moreover, it was hardly possible that any woman would be allowed to approach the altar. Not without wonder, he awaited the outcome. Christina spoke, 'Rest assured that my flesh is free from all corruption.' And once she had spoken she disappeared.

Filled with gladness, and hardly able to contain himself for joy, he duly finished the mass but was unable to put as quick an end to his ardent desire to honour the virgin. Finding one of the monks of St Albans, who by chance had come to Bermondsey at the time, he sent a message to Abbot Geoffrey through the same monk telling him what he had seen, what he had heard, and what he knew for certain about Christina. And as the monk was one of those who slandered her, the Lord in his mercy and justice had arranged that through this message he should become aware of what he ought to feel about Christina; so that, if he should in future spread any false rumour about her, he would not be left in doubt that he was acting against his conscience, and would be harshly judged and punished as a false tale-bearer. But the venerable Simon was quite unaware that the monk was such a one. When the abbot received Simon's message he gave many thanks to God, since he mercifully revealed to others what he himself already knew.

Christina, incapable of being crushed by the cunning of the devil, since by the shield of faith she had already warded off many serious attacks, wondered what new offering she could make to God in order to enlighten the abbot and put an end to the shamelessness of her detractors, whom she pitied. So, lit by a flame that never burns out, she proposed to offer every Sunday night in the church the gift of a wax candle. The sisters agreed to the proposal, though they did not know why it was being suggested. It was then Saturday. The devil, irritated by the virgin's constancy, which he could not inwardly disturb by his or his followers' attempts, tried to frighten her outwardly by assuming a monstrous appearance. And so on the following night, that is to say, towards daybreak on Sunday, while Christina was in the monastery and while the others were getting ready for matins, they saw a body without a head, for the devil had lost God, his head. He was sitting in the cloister near the entrance of the church. When they saw this, girlish terror overtook them and they fell at the foot of their mistress. You could see one trying to bury herself in her bosom, another trying to hide under her veil, another clinging to her knees, another cowering at her feet; one hiding under a bench and another lying on the ground, trembling as if she was about to breathe her last. To all this there was but one remedy, to touch Christina's garments. The devil, no less bold, burst into the church. At the sight of this monster Christina was somewhat afraid, but gaining courage she turned to the Lord and poured out prayers and thrust out that monstrous phantom. But for some time afterwards a more than ordinary terror swept over her. Deeply grieved at this she poured out prayers and lamentations to him in whom she had placed her trust, worrying that if she began to fear the monstrous appearances of the devil this meant that God was deserting her. She prayed often and persistently on this matter, until this answer was given to her: 'These particular prayers are not necessary, but you should know that the prayers for your beloved friend that he be enlightened with eternal light have certainly been granted. However, the frightful images and the envy of your detractors you must understand will soon be checked. Though the demon inwardly rages and outwardly sharpens the tongues of your detractors you must not cease from doing good nor lose constancy in times of adversity.'

Encouraged by these replies, and gladdened at the same time by the assurance of her friend's salvation, she began to examine more often and more closely in the depths of her heart whether anyone can love another more than himself, at least in matters that pertain to the love of God. While she was preoccupied with this, and was one day praying longer than usual in her monastery, she was suddenly overcome with such joy that she could not understand it, nor would she have been able to describe it to anyone. She was in a state of elation for some time, and as she was communing with God she heard (not in words but in her mind) this voice in the sanctuary of her heart. 'He whom you love so much for my sake, for whose salvation you continue to intercede, would you like him to suffer the straits of death for my sake?'

Crying inwardly, but with a great surge of feeling, she replied in a broken voice, 'Gladly, O Lord, and if thy will were plain, I would carry it out with my own hands. For if Abraham showed his devotion to you through the pledge of his only son,* why should not I, if you ordered it, slay him for your sake? All the more since the love which bound him to his son was carnal although not in opposition to yours, while the love which binds me to him you alone know. What death is more glorious than that undertaken out of love for the creator? What life is more joyful than that honourably lived through grace?'

As she continued in these reciprocal but solitary, sweet but indescribable conversations with God, she was keenly aware of a prod on her right side, which nonetheless did not hurt her, as if someone said, 'Look!' And as she looked towards the altar she saw sweet Jesus with the expression and stance of one who has compassion on sinners. And turning her eyes, she saw her close friend for whom she was anxious standing at her right side,* which was the Lord's left side. And when they knelt to pray, as the virgin's left was on the Lord's right (for they were facing opposite ways), fearing lest he should be at the Lord's left, she began to wonder how he could be transferred to the right, feeling it intolerable that her beloved should not be nearer to the Lord's right than she was, since she thought that the right side was more honourable. However, she did not want to be lifted over her beloved, who was prostrate in prayer, but to be carried across in some other way. And while she was moved by this desire she suddenly understood that the right hand, which she wanted to be merciful in all things and above all things, was indeed hers. And so, during their many uplifting conversations, she used to tell her friend that there was only one thing in which a person should not place another before him or herself, and that was God's love.

One day a certain pilgrim,* quite unknown but of reverend appearance, came to the cell of the virgin Christina. She welcomed him hospitably as she did everyone, not asking him any questions, nor at the time did he tell her who he was. So he went on his way, leaving a deep impression on her memory. After a time he returned. First he made an offering of prayers to the Lord; thereafter he took pleasure in talking to Christina. During the conversation Christina, feeling a divine fervour, recognized that her visitor stood out among men and that he was in a class of his own. Much delighted by this, she urged him as an act of kindness to take some food. He sat at the table while she and her sister Margaret prepared the meal, but Christina paid more attention to the man while Margaret bustled around preoccupied with all that needed doing, so that supposing it had been possible to see Jesus sitting down, you would have recognized another Mary and another Martha.* And so, when the table was ready, the pilgrim raised bread to his mouth and looked as if he was about to eat. But had you been there, you would have noticed that he tasted rather than ate. And when invited to take a little bit of the fish set before him, he said that there was no need to take more than his poor body required. And while both sisters were admiring the attractiveness of his features, his handsome beard, his distinguished appearance, and his thoughtful words, they were filled with such spiritual joy that they felt they had before them an angel rather than a man, and, if their virginal modesty had allowed, they would have asked him to stay. But after giving them a blessing and taking his leave of them, he set out on his way, still known to the sisters only by sight. On the other hand, so deep an impression did his manner leave on their hearts, so much sweetness did he instil in them, that often, when they were speaking together, they would say, with sighs that showed their feelings, 'If only our pilgrim would return, if only we could enjoy further conversation with him. If only we could see him again and learn more from his fine and distinguished example.' They often encouraged each other to yearn for the man in this way.

As she thought these things over, Christina prepared herself for the coming of the feast of Christmas, uncertain, however, where her yearnings would take her. On the day before the vigil of the feast she was ill and had to keep to her bed; indeed, she was so weak that on the vigil she could not go to church. When they heard this two monks, god-fearing men, visited her as an act of kindness. And while they were chanting the hours of the Christmas vigil to the virgin as she lay in her bed, she particularly noted among all that she heard the versicle of the hour of none, the special joy of that particular

84

feast: 'Today ye shall know that the Lord will come and tomorrow ye shall see his glory.'* On realizing the significance of the verse, she was moved with such spiritual joy that for the rest of the day and the following night thoughts of this kind kept running through her mind: 'Oh, at what hour will the Lord come? How will he come? Who will see him when he comes? Who will deserve to see his glory? What will that glory be like? And how great will be the joy of those who see it?' Fixing her mind on holy desires of this kind, confined as she was to bed with a severe illness, she prepared herself for the hour of matins. As she heard the [anthem] proper to the feast, 'Christ is born', she understood that she had been invited to the joy of his birth. Her illness entirely disappeared and she was filled with such spiritual joy that she could think of nothing but divine things. And when the others sang the hymn *Te Deum laudamus*,* she looked up and felt as if she had been borne into the church of St Albans and that she was standing on the steps of the lectern where the lessons for matins are read. And as she looked down on the choir, she saw someone in the middle of the choir looking with pleasure at the sight of the monks singing. It would have been impossible for anyone to describe his beauty. On his head he bore a golden crown thickly encrusted with precious stones which seemed to excel any work of human skill. On the top was a cross of gold of wonderful craftsmanship, not so much made by man as by God. Hanging down from his head on either side were two bands or fillets attached to the crown, delicate and shining, and on the tops of the gems it looked as if there was dew. In this guise appeared the man whose beauty had only to be seen to be loved, for he is the fairest of the children of men.* And when Christina had gazed on his beauty, she felt herself rapt in some way to another world. But whether she saw these things in the body or out of the body* (God is her witness), she never knew. On the day after Christmas, when it was nearly time for the procession, a message was brought to her that the pilgrim for whom she longed had arrived. When she heard this, her joy was unbounded and added fire to the flames of her desire. For she hoped to profit greatly from providing a meal to the person who, in the shape of her pilgrim, had by his presence so sweetly revived and nourished her. And so she ordered the doors to be closed.

The pilgrim, then, followed the procession as it set out; his unassuming demeanour as he walked, the solemnity of his expression, and the gentleness of his appearance were evident and set an example of dignity to the virgins' choir, following the Scriptures, 'I will give thee thanks in the great congregation.'* After the procession, the pilgrim took part with everyone at mass. When the service had ended, the virgin of Christ went ahead of the others. Her longing for the pilgrim knew no bounds, so she left the church in order to be the first to greet him as he came out. The only way of leaving was by going past her. The pilgrim took his time; this was tantalizing to the virgin. When everyone else had come out, she asked, 'Where is the pilgrim?'

'Oh,' they said, 'he is praying in the church.'

The delay made her impatient and she sent people to summon him. When they returned they said that they could not find him anywhere. The virgin was astonished and asked with concern, 'Where is the key of the door?'

'Look, here it is,' said the person to whom it had been entrusted. 'From the moment mass began, no one could have come out since the door has been locked and I have guarded the key.'

Nor indeed had anyone seen him come out of the church. Who else could we say he was except an angel or the Lord Jesus? For he who had appeared that night in such a guise showed himself in some measure as he will be seen in glory. For this is how that glory appears to us in this present life, since we see it only through a glass.* Hence God is said to dwell in darkness;* not that he dwells in darkness, but his light, because of its brightness, blinds us who are weighed down by the body. On that day he wished to be seen as a pilgrim, indeed as a man in the prime of his life.

However, nothing is lacking to those who fear God nor to those who love him in truth: 'Behold, O Lord, you have loved truth; the unascertained and hidden elements of your wisdom you have made known to me.'* Among such your handmaid Christina shone out, for the closer she got to you in true love, the more clearly was she able to see the hidden elements of your wisdom with her pure heart. Hence you gave her the power to know the secret thoughts of men and to see those that were far off and deliberately hidden as if they were present. This can be seen in what follows. One of her servants was thinking of doing something (I do not know what) secretly, which the handmaid of God, seated in another house, saw through the walls and forbade her to do, saying: 'Don't. Do not do it.'

The girl said, 'What, my lady?' and she said, 'What you were just thinking'.

'But,' said the girl, 'I wasn't thinking of anything that was forbidden.'

Then Christina called her to her and whispered in her ear what she had seen her turning over in her heart. On hearing this, the girl blushed deeply with shame, a proof that Christina spoke the truth. She begged and implored Christina for the sake of her good name not to tell anyone, because she would never be able to bear the disgrace of it were it to be revealed.

On another occasion, as we were sitting at table with the handmaid of Christ, the same servant produced a dish for us to eat. We ate some of it, but Christina refused to touch it. We asked her to share the dish with us but she would not do so, and called for Godgifu, for that was the girl's name.

She asked her quietly (out of respect for the guests) if she had made the dish with any of the forbidden herbs, for Christina had been emphatic that for a time she would eat nothing from the garden next door because the owner, out of miserliness, had denied her a sprig of chervil when she had recently asked for it. In the meantime she helped herself to some of the dish without comment but did not taste it. After the meal she soon proved the guilt of the girl by the testimony of those who had seen her, and the girl confessed that what they had eaten had been gathered in the forbidden garden.

This virgin had a certain friend who loved her very much . . . by her servant she sent him certain things which . . . but the servant pilfered some of them on the way and used them for his own evil ends. When the virgin of God saw this with her spiritual eyes she confronted him and privately rebuked him, cleansing him of his guilt.

Christina had a sister who was living in the world and was called Matilda. As she and her husband were lying in bed one night in Huntingdon, for that is where they lived, Christina in her cell saw and heard them talking, so that when later they came to visit her, she was able to relate in detail what they had said, at what time and where. Both of them admitted to me that all this happened as she said.

Night and day Christina kept in her mind her dear friend Abbot Geoffrey, whom we have mentioned above. For his sake she ceaselessly fasted, prayed, and called upon God, the angels, and all the saints in heaven and earth, beseeching God with prayers and supplications for his mercy and wisely rebuking the abbot whenever he seemed to act in ways that were not quite right . . .

EXPLANATORY NOTES

3 *Auti . . . Beatrix*: for the significance of naming patterns after the Conquest see the Introduction, p. vii.

Theodora: lit. 'Gift of God'. Theodora is an unusual name in this period and may have been chosen for its symbolism.

the monastery . . . in the town: this is likely to be the Augustinian priory of St Mary's, Huntingdon, founded sometime between 1086 and 1092; it later moved outside the town.

between the Feast of the Assumption and the Nativity of Our Lady: i.e. between 15 August and 8 September.

Such a sign . . . sevenfold grace: the Holy Spirit appeared in the form of a dove at Christ's baptism (Matthew 3: 16; Mark 1: 10; Luke 3: 32; John 1: 32). The prophet Isaiah foresees Christ as filled with a sevenfold grace: wisdom, understanding, counsel, might, knowledge, piety, and fear of the Lord (Isaiah 11: 2–3).

4 *matins and the remaining hours, and mass*: the life of any monastery revolved around the singing of psalms at the seven daily services (nocturns, matins, prime, terce, sext, none, vespers). Regional and seasonal variations notwithstanding, the hours, beginning with nocturns, might have been observed at 3 a.m., 6 a.m., 6.45 a.m., 8 a.m., 12 noon, 1.30 p.m., 4.15 p.m. For Beatrix to have attended the services mentioned in the text and given birth before terce, an exceptionally short labour must be imagined.

St Leonard: a hermit, who lived in the sixth century, and was subsequently favoured by hermits; allegedly, he helped Clothtilda, the wife of the Frankish King Clovis, give birth, though his cult dates from the mid-eleventh century. For the choice of St Leonard over St Winnocus, whom the Anglo-Saxons venerated on 6 November, see Thomas Head, 'The Marriages of Christina of Markyate', in Samuel Fanous and Henrietta Leyser, *Christina of Markyate: A Twelfth-Century Holy Woman* (Abingdon and New York, 2005), 122.

love righteousness and hate iniquity: Psalm 45: 7.

small girl . . .: omissions marked in the text indicate missing or illegible passages in the fire-damaged manuscript (see the Note on the Text and Translation).

5 *blessed martyr Alban*: martyred in AD 215. Alban is Britain's protomartyr. At the time of Christina's visit the abbey was being rebuilt. The new church was consecrated in 1116 by Henry I.

5 *the sign of the cross*: holy graffiti was not unusual in churches frequented by pilgrims.

Shillington: a village 25 miles from Huntingdon and 17 miles from St Albans. According to the Ramsey Cartulary, a certain Auti of Huntingdon had rights over the church in Shillington. See Rachel Koopmans, 'Dining at Markyate', in Fanous and Leyser, *Christina of Markyate*, 143–59.

6 *Lord . . . from Thee*: Psalm 38: 9.

Whom . . . works: Psalm 73: 25–8.

I offer this penny: ritual gifts were intended to symbolize expressions of loyalty and allegiance. See Thomas Head, 'The Marriages of Christina of Markyate', in Fanous and Leyser, *Christina of Markyate*, 116–37.

her Sueno: this is a literal translation of the Latin, *Sueno suo*, and is evidently meant to suggest a degree of intimacy between Christina and Sueno.

Ranulf: Ranulf was justiciar (chief minister) of England until his appointment as bishop of Durham in 1099. While rules on clerical celibacy were being tightened in the twelfth century, concubinage among priests was still frequent. For Ranulf's career see Frank Barlow, 'Ranulf (d. 1123)', *Oxford Dictionary of National Biography* (Oxford, 2004) [http://www.oxforddnb.com/view/article/23048, accessed 30 Aug. 2007].

7 *put into his heart*: John 13: 2.

8 *to arrange his betrothal*: on twelfth-century marriage law, see the Introduction (p. x) and Head, 'The Marriages of Christina of Markyate,' in Fanous and Leyser, *Christina of Markyate*, 116–37.

10 *evil communications corrupt good manners*: 1 Corinthians 15: 33.

Gild merchant: gilds, associations formed for 'mutual aid, religious acts, fellowship, and drinking', have Anglo-Saxon origins; see R. Bartlett, *England Under the Norman and Angevin Kings, 1075–1225* (Oxford, 2000), 239.

11 *Hail Mary*: a form of prayer based on the angel Gabriel's greeting to Mary (Luke 1: 28).

St Cecilia . . . Valerian: St Cecilia allegedly lived in the second or third century and was responsible for the conversion of her husband Valerian, whom she followed in martyrdom. The story of Cecilia, who persuaded her husband to live chastely with her, circulated in pre-Conquest England, and is likely to have been more familiar to Christina than the Norman story of Alexis, which also features a chaste marriage, and was later included in the St Albans Psalter, a book associated with Christina. See Thomas Head, 'The Marriages of Christina of Markyate', in Fanous and Leyser, *Christina of Markyate*, 122.

12 *if we suffer with them we shall also reign with them*: cf. Romans 8: 17 and 2 Timothy 2: 12.

13 *Let them be turned backward . . . hurt*: Psalm 70: 3.

14 *the lowliness of his handmaiden*: Luke 1: 48.

   how are they increased that trouble me: Psalm 3: 1.

   I have looked . . . but I found none: Psalm 69: 20.

15 *Unto Thee . . . my soul*: Psalm 25: 1.

   Blessed are ye . . . great in heaven: Luke 6: 22–3.

   Christina: a fourth-century martyr beaten by her father and imprisoned.

   obedient . . . death: Philippians 2: 8.

16 *marry in the Lord*: 1 Corinthians 7: 39.

17 *For this . . . one flesh*: Mark 10: 7–9.

   let not the husband put away the wife: 1 Corinthians 7: 3–4, 10–11.

   And we know . . . in the Old and New Testaments: e.g. Exodus 20: 12, 14; Colossians 3: 20.

   mothers of families are saved: from early times, the Church favoured the state of virginity more highly than marriage or widowhood. The fact that the Fourth Lateran Council in 1215 decreed that married people as well as virgins could be saved suggests a need to combat a lingering doubt as to whether the gates of heaven would be open to the married.

18 *Every one who leaves . . . eternal life*: Matthew 19: 29.

19 *carrying red hot irons . . . bare hands*: The truth of any statement could be legally tested through 'trial by ordeal'. See Robert Bartlett, *Trial by Fire and Water: The Medieval Judicial Process* (Oxford, 1986).

   Buckden: this was a residence of the bishops of Lincoln. Robert became chancellor in 1091 and bishop of Lincoln in 1094. See Dorothy M. Owen, 'Bloet, Robert (*d.* 1123)', *Oxford Dictionary of National Biography* (Oxford, 2004) [http://www.oxforddnb.com/view/articles/26365, accessed 5 Dec. 2006].

20 *Robert the dean*: a Robert, priest of Huntingdon, witnessed the agreement in which Auti gave back the church of Shillington to the abbot of Ramsey between 1114 and 1123 for 10 marks of silver.

22 *generous provision*: in the early twelfth century any woman entering a monastery was still expected to provide the equivalent of a dowry, though this practice was discontinued later in the century.

23 *this last judgement . . . false*: given that the inverse is true, this may be an ironical remark or an instance of scribal error.

Joseph: a reference to the story of Joseph, whom Potiphar's wife attempted to seduce but who fled when seized, leaving behind his garment in her hands (Genesis 39: 7–20).

24 *naked go and follow Christ*: this much-quoted phrase is first recorded in the letters of St Jerome (*c*.340–420), *Letter* 52.5.

25 *ridicule . . . deliver you from their hands*: a conflation of Jeremiah 20: 7, Luke 19: 43, and Psalm 31: 15.

26 *Judith*: a type of the anchoress, later invoked in the *Ancrene Wisse* (ed. Anne Savage and Nicholas Watson, The Classics of Western Spirituality (Mahawah, NJ, 1991), 96–7).

The immense joy . . . of her expression: for a discussion of this vision see Barbara Newman, 'What Did it Mean to say "I Saw"? The Clash between Theory and Practice in Medieval Visionary Culture', *Speculum*, 80 (2005), 1–43 at 21.

28 *Roger*: little is known of Roger, but his tomb survives to this day in St Albans. The *Rule of St Benedict* had always envisaged that some monks, after serving a term of probation in the monastery, might choose to become hermits.

30 *the archbishop was Ralph*: Ralph d'Escures, archbishop of Canterbury, 1114–22. See 'Ralph d'Escures (*c*.1068–1122)', *Oxford Dictionary of National Biography* (Oxford, 2004) [http://www.oxforddnb.com/view/article/23047, accessed 30 Aug. 2007].

32 *reeve*: a local official of minor rank.

33 *please my husband*: 1 Corinthians 7: 34.

dog to its vomit: Proverbs 26: 11.

35 *Lord, all my desire . . . seeking her life*: Psalm 38: 9, 11–12.

in holiness . . . all the days of her life: Luke 1: 75.

the anchorites of Huntingdon: the list of hermits and anchorites in medieval England (including Huntingdon), identified by R. M. Clay in 1914, is being updated by E. A. Jones. See 'The Hermits and Anchorites of England', in Fanous and Leyser, *Christina of Markyate*, 229–39.

36 *the Lord who made heaven . . . Zion*: Psalm 134: 3.

39 *rooted and grounded in the love of God*: Ephesians 3: 17.

one in heart and soul: Acts 4: 32.

40 *a span-and-a-half*: the span was traditionally the distance between the tip of the thumb and the tip of the little finger when the hand is outstretched.

42 *our Lord's annunciation*: 25 March, another witness to the significance of Marian dates in Christina's text.

fairest of the children of men . . . Jerusalem must carry this cross: Psalm 45: 2. Jerusalem was the ultimate pilgrimage destination in the Middle Ages, but also a metaphor for the heavenly city. This passage combines a number of different images, notably the Annunciation and the Harrowing of Hell. See Elizabeth Petroff, *Medieval Women's Visionary Literature* (Oxford, 1986), 137–8.

myn sunendaege dohter: this is the only use of Anglo-Saxon in the *Life*, a poignant reminder of Christina's native language and culture. During Christina's lifetime the *Anglo-Saxon Chronicle* was still being maintained at Peterborough, not far from Christina's hometown, though the last entry for this was 1155.

rose from the dead: 27 March is the traditional date of Easter in the Middle Ages. However, in 1122 Easter fell on 26 March, and given the way that dates were calculated in the Middle Ages, it may be that this is the actual date of the event. It is possible that Christina retained a document made on that day confirming that her vows had been annulled. We owe this suggestion to Tom Licence.

44 *Thurstan of York*: Thurstan was archbishop of York from 1114 until his death in February 1140; see Janet Burton, 'Thurstan (*c*.1070–1140)', *Oxford Dictionary of National Biography* (Oxford, 2004) [http://www.oxforddnb.com/view/articles/27/27411, accessed 6 Dec. 2006].

Caddington: a village lying 2 miles to the north of Markyate.

45 *Redbourn*: a village some 4 miles from Markyate, along the Roman road towards St Albans and London. It is the site of the cell of St Albans which owned the only surviving copy of Christina's life. This passage is taken from the *Gesta Abbatum* (*Deeds of the Abbots*), 1.100, where the corresponding excerpt from the *Life* occurs. The image of a holy woman on the altar screen of the church, *puella* (maiden) *de Redbourn*, may be a reference to Christina.

from that moment into his keeping: John 19: 27.

apostolic indult: a licence or permission granted by the pope.

46 *pollute the wax*: very often writers composed a first draft of their work on wax tablets.

47 *the devil*: C. H. Talbot, in his edition, supplied the word 'cleric' (*clericus*) at this point for the missing text. However, 'devil' (*diabolus*) seems more likely, as there are other instances in medieval lives of devils manifesting themselves as shaggy bears, whereas there are no known instances of clerics dressing up as bears. We owe this suggestion to Tom Licence.

47 *Benedict the founder of monks*: Benedict of Nursia, the sixth-century monk of Monte Casino to whom the *Rule of St Benedict* is attributed, which from the ninth century became the standard monastic rule in the West.

48 *lowly estate of his handmaid*: Luke 1: 48.

sacrifice of thanksgiving: Psalm 116: 17.

49 *the falling sickness*: this is likely to have been epilepsy.

virgin Margaret: St Margaret of Antioch, whose martyrdom is traditionally associated with the persecutions against Christians in the fourth century, was a saint much favoured by women. Vernacular versions of her life circulated in Anglo-Saxon England.

canon of the mass: the most solemn part of the mass including the consecration.

51 *rested on the seventh day*: i.e. Saturday (Genesis 2: 2).

52 *the virgins . . . gathered together . . . at York*: at the convent of St Clement, founded between 1125 and 1135.

Marcigny: Marcigny-les-Nonnains, founded in 1080 by St Hugh of Cluny. It housed two kinds of nuns: those living in community and those living as recluses in separate cells.

Fontevrault: founded by Robert d'Arbrissel, *c*.1100, for women who had previously lived under his direction.

Roger . . . was buried there: Roger's tomb is still visible in St Albans Abbey.

certain souls: this is likely to be a reference to Abbot Geoffrey, though Talbot believed it to be a later abbot, Robert Gorham (1151–66).

53 *Assumption of the Mother of God*: 15 August.

days of the festival: major liturgical festivals were commemorated throughout the week that followed, culminating in the octave (i.e. the eighth day) of the festival.

nocturns: the first of the seven monastic hours of the day, cf. above, note to p. 4.

55 *prayed for those who cursed her*: Luke 6: 28.

darts . . . shield of faith: Ephesians 6: 16.

56 *no man to be tempted beyond his strength*: 1 Corinthians 10: 13.

Abbot Geoffrey of St Albans: Geoffrey of Gorron, from Le Mans, came to England at the invitation of Abbot Robert too late to take up the post of master of St Albans School, becoming instead a teacher at Dunstable. Here, he put on a play of St Katherine for which he borrowed copes from the abbey of St Albans. When these were burned in a fire in his house, he offered himself as a 'burnt offering' to St Albans, becoming a monk and subsequently the abbot in 1119. See James G. Clark, 'Gorham, Geoffrey de (*c*.1100–1146)', *Oxford Dictionary of National Biography* (Oxford, 2004) [http://www.oxforddnb.com/view/articles/10529, accessed 6 Dec. 2006].

59 *it is not ye . . . in you*: Matthew 10: 20.

the shadow of him whom lovers find: Song of Songs 2: 3. Bede's commentary on the Song of Songs was illustrated by the Alexis Master in the early twelfth century at St Albans (Cambridge, Kings College, MS. 19). It is remarkable for its eroticism in the portrayal of Christ and the bride of the Song. In the twelfth century the bride could be taken to represent the individual soul, though some commentators suggested that she was the Virgin Mary.

60 *wounds of a friend . . . an enemy*: Proverbs 27: 6.

God . . . receives: Hebrews 12: 6.

61 *Margaret the sister of Christina*: Margaret's death is recorded in the calendar of the St Albans Psalter.

having said Benedicite: the reference is to the monastic custom of saying *Benedicite* (a blessing) before entering upon any conversation. As soon as the Superior, or whoever was addressed, had answered *Dominus* ('Lord'), the conversation could begin.

62 *Pentecost*: feast commemorating the descent of the Holy Spirit on the Church, described in Acts 2.

63 *feast of St Matthew*: 21 September.

Alexander, bishop of Lincoln: bishop from 1123 to 1148. See David M. Smith, 'Alexander (*d*.1148), bishop of Lincoln', *Oxford Dictonary of National Biography* (Oxford, 2004) [http://www.oxforddnb.com/view/article/324, accessed 30 Aug. 2007].

Epiphany: the feast, on 6 January, commemorating the visit of the Magi to the infant Christ. See Matthew 2: 11ff. For octave, see above note to p. 53.

scourge: a recognized form of self-inflicted penitential discipline in the monastic tradition, taken to extremes by the Flagellants in the late Middle Ages.

65 *a red cope*: the use of liturgical colours was not yet rigidly fixed. Red is the colour generally associated with passion, and its use here may signal a turning-point in the relationship between Geoffrey and Christina.

66 *having nothing and possessing all things*: 2 Corinthians 6: 10. The evidence of the *Deeds of the Abbots* supports the view that Geoffrey was generous to hermits or recluses.

67 *which happened to be a camilla*: Lat. *Camomilla*, Camomile.

 the wise and prudent: Matthew 11: 25.

68 *blessed Gregory*: this is likely to be Gregory the Great (*c*.540–604), author of the *Dialogues*, a collection of stories about the lives and miracles of Italian saints.

 This is . . . wonderful in our eyes: Matthew 21: 42.

69 *a dove*: here is another instance of the dove as symbol of the Holy Spirit (see above, p. 3).

71 *viaticum*: originally, the money required for a journey; in ecclesiastical usage, the Eucharist administered to those about to die.

 king of England: when Henry I died in 1135 Stephen was elected king, despite the barons' earlier promise to elect Henry's daughter Matilda to the throne. Stephen was crowned the following year. The dispute that followed led to civil war.

 Pope Innocent II: pope from 1130 to 1143.

 undergarments: needlework was commonly undertaken by cloistered women. Christina also made slippers given to Pope Adrian IV, whose father had been a monk at St Albans.

72 *the venerable Thomas*: in fact, Thomas has not been mentioned. This is one of a number of clues suggesting that the text has not been revised.

 general council: the Second Lateran Council, convened by Pope Innocent II in 1139 for the reformation of the Church, followed a disputed election to the papacy.

73 *Roman legate*: legates were papal deputies, entrusted with the pope's authority.

74 *Theobald*: archbishop from 1139 to 1161. See Frank Barlow, 'Theobald (*c*.1090–1161), archbishop of Canterbury', *Oxford Dictionary of National Biography* (Oxford, 2004) [http://www.oxforddnb.com/view/articles/27168, accessed 6 Dec. 2006].

 Roger of Salisbury . . . Alexander of Lincoln: for Alexander, see above, note to p. 63. Roger of Salisbury was bishop from 1102 to 1139. For Roger's career and the arrest of the bishops, see B. R. Kemp, 'Salisbury, Roger of (*d*.1139)', *Oxford Dictionary of National Biography* (Oxford, 2004) [http://www.oxforddnb.com/view/articles/23956, accessed 6 Dec. 2006].

 Henry, bishop of Winchester: bishop from 1129 to 1171.

75 *excommunication*: the sentence of excommunication was the ultimate sanction the Church could impose, depriving the individual of the sacraments and placing him or her outside the Church's protection.

77 *Evianus*: possibly the same as Evisandus; as above, p. 66.

 the sacrament: where possible, the dying penitent made his or her confession and received the Eucharist.

78 *perverse generation*: Matthew 17: 17.

 women about with them: 1 Corinthians 9: 5.

 savour of Christ: 2 Corinthians 2: 16.

79 *Jerome . . . Paula*: a reference to the relationship between St Jerome and St Paula, widow and mother of St Eustochium. Paula presided over a convent of nuns founded by St Jerome at Bethlehem. Jerome and Paula's friendship was the object of gossip, inviting parallels between Geoffrey and Christina.

 Zabulus: a name of the devil.

 Simon: the name Simon means 'he who hears'.

82 *Abraham . . . his only son*: for the story of Abraham and the Sacrifice of Isaac, see Genesis 22: 1–19.

83 *right side*: in many societies, the right hand symbolizes preferment and honour.

 a certain pilgrim: this pilgrim can be understood as Christ himself, who appeared after the Resurrection to his disciples on the road to Emmaus (Luke 24: 13–32). The Emmaus story is illustrated in three scenes in the St Albans Psalter. See Neil Cartlidge, 'The Unknown Pilgrim: Drama and Romance in *The Life of Christina of Markyate*', in Fanous and Leyser, *Christina of Markyate*, 79–98.

84 *Mary and another Martha*: they attended Jesus when he visited the home of Lazarus (Luke 10: 38–42; John 11–12: 9), and were interpreted allegorically as representing the contemplative and active life respectively.

85 *Today . . . his glory*: cf. Exodus 16: 6–7.

 Te Deum laudamus: 'We praise Thee, O God', a Latin hymn of praise attributed, since the ninth century, to SS Ambrose and Augustine.

 the fairest of the children of men: see above, note to p. 42.

 in the body or out of the body: 2 Corinthians 12: 2–3.

86 *I will give thee thanks in the great congregation*: Psalm 35: 18.

87 *through a glass*: 1 Corinthians 13: 12.

 to dwell in darkness: 2 Chronicles 6: 1.

 Behold . . . made known to me: Psalm 51: 6.

INDEX

Index

Lincoln 23

London 7, 8, 79

Loric 33

Marcigny xii, 52

Margaret (sister to Christina) xiii, 61, 62, 63, 68, 71, 83

Margaret, St 49

Markyate viii, xiii, xvi, xvii, xxi, xxv, xxvi

Martin, St xxii

Mary (BV), St xi, xv, xx, 3, 4, 11, 25, 27, 43, 44, 52, 53, 70

Mary Magdalen 47

Mary and Martha xv

Matilda/Eadgifu, queen vii

Matilda (sister to Christina) 3, 34, 88

Melisen 9

Northumbria 7

Oxford 74

Paul, St xx

Paula 79

Peter, St 15

Ralph, archbishop of Canterbury 30

Ranulf Flambard, bishop of Durham vii, viii, ix, xxii, 6, 7, 8, 23

Redbourn 45

Reginald of Durham xxv

Robert, dean of Huntingdon 20, 43

Robert Bloet, bishop of Lincoln 19, 22, 23, 46, 48

Robert de Gorron, abbot of St Albans xxv

Robert of Flamstead, priest 43

Roger, bishop of Salisbury 74

Roger the hermit viii, xvi, xvii, xx, xxii, 28, 29, 31, 35, 36, 38, 39, 40, 41, 42, 43, 44, 45, 52

Rome x, 71, 72, 73, 75

St Albans viii, ix, xii, xiii, xiv, xv, xxi, xxii, xxiv, xxv, 49, 71, 80, 85

St Paul's, London xiii

Shillington 5

Simon of Bermondsey 79, 80

Stephen, king 71, 72, 74, 75, 76

Sueno xvii, 4, 5, 6, 14, 16, 22, 26, 27, 32, 36

Talbot, C. H., xxiii, xxvii

Theobald, archbishop of Canterbury 74

Theodora (Christina) 3, 15, 16, 33, 34, 43

Thomas 72

Thurstan, archbishop of York xviii, 44, 45, 52

Valerian, St 11

Watton xvii

Westminster 61

William Rufus, king vii

William the Conqueror, king vii

Winchester 74

Windsor 28

Wulfwine 36

York xii, 52

Zabulus 79

Bhagavad Gita

The Bible Authorized King James Version
With Apocrypha

Dhammapada

Dharmasūtras

The Koran

The Pañcatantra

The Sauptikaparvan (from the
Mahabharata)

The Tale of Sinuhe and Other Ancient
Egyptian Poems

The Qur'an

Upaniṣads

ANSELM OF CANTERBURY   The Major Works

THOMAS AQUINAS   Selected Philosophical Writings

AUGUSTINE   The Confessions
On Christian Teaching

BEDE   The Ecclesiastical History

HEMACANDRA   The Lives of the Jain Elders

KĀLIDĀSA   The Recognition of Śakuntalā

MANJHAN   Madhumalati

ŚĀNTIDEVA   The Bodhicaryàvatàra

	Late Victorian Gothic Tales
JANE AUSTEN	Emma
	Mansfield Park
	Persuasion
	Pride and Prejudice
	Selected Letters
	Sense and Sensibility
MRS BEETON	Book of Household Management
MARY ELIZABETH BRADDON	Lady Audley's Secret
ANNE BRONTË	The Tenant of Wildfell Hall
CHARLOTTE BRONTË	Jane Eyre
	Shirley
	Villette
EMILY BRONTË	Wuthering Heights
ROBERT BROWNING	The Major Works
JOHN CLARE	The Major Works
SAMUEL TAYLOR COLERIDGE	The Major Works
WILKIE COLLINS	The Moonstone
	No Name
	The Woman in White
CHARLES DARWIN	The Origin of Species
THOMAS DE QUINCEY	The Confessions of an English Opium-Eater
	On Murder
CHARLES DICKENS	The Adventures of Oliver Twist
	Barnaby Rudge
	Bleak House
	David Copperfield
	Great Expectations
	Nicholas Nickleby
	The Old Curiosity Shop
	Our Mutual Friend
	The Pickwick Papers